Answers 1-4

Essential Music Theory

Mark Sarnecki

San Marco Publications

Elementary Music Theory © 2023 by San Marco Publications. All rights reserved.

All right reserved. No part of this book may be reproduced in any form or by electronic or mechanical means including Information storage and retrieval systems without permission in writing from the author.

ISNB: 1-896499-41-4

Contents

Level 1:	1
Level 2:	28
Level 3:	51
Level 4:	82

Level 1

Page 8, No. 1

F D B A E E
G F C A B D
E D C B A G
F E A F C D

Page 10, No. 1

B G E D A A
G F C A B D
A G F E D C
A G C A E F

Page 12, No. 1

B C A G B C
B C B D D E
D A F B D C
C D E D E C
A D B B F G

Page 13, No. 2

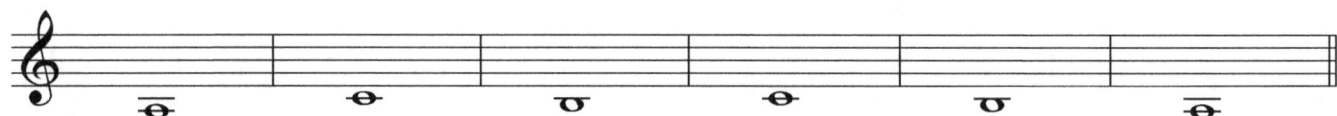

Page 13, No. 3

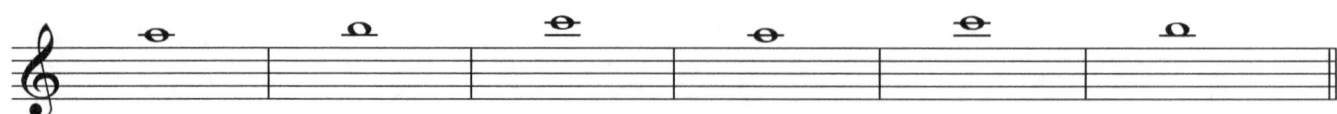

Page 13, No. 4

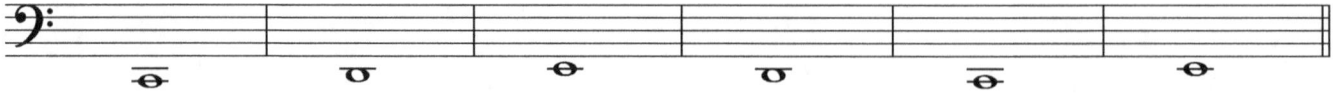

Page 13, No. 5

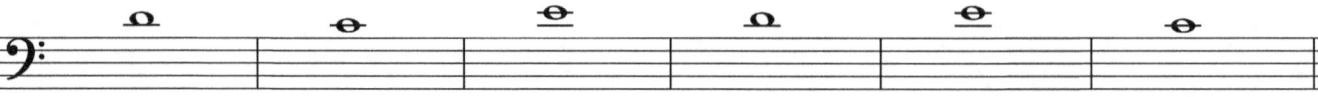

Page 13, No. 6

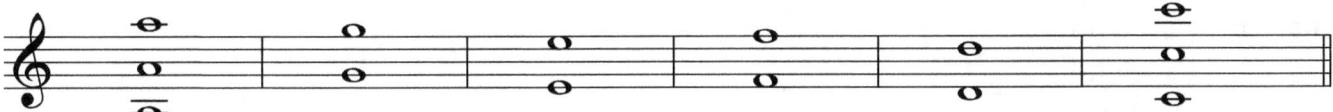

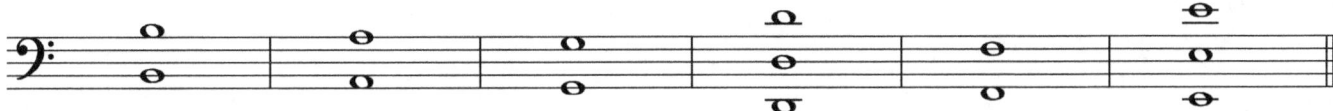

Page 14, No. 1
F C F B A D E C
E D B F G A C C

Page 14, No. 2

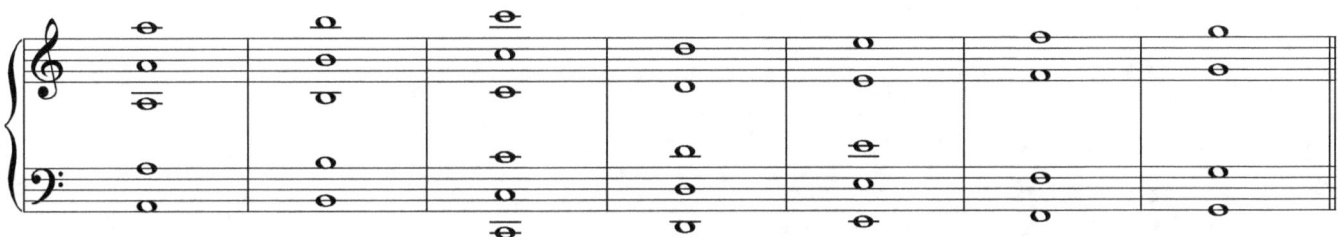

Page 15, No. 3
C B F E D A
B G D C F E

Page 16, other choices are possible

©San Marco Publications 2022   Level 1

Page 21, No. 1

quarter	eighth
half	eighth
whole	dotted half

Page 21, No. 2

1	1
2	4
1/2	3

Page 22, No. 3

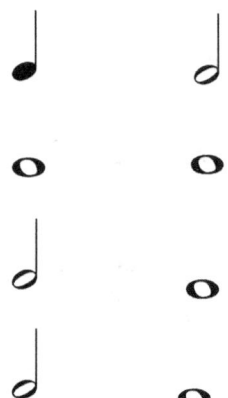

Page 23, No. 1

Page 26, No. 5

quarter note	eighth rest
half rest	whole rest
whole note	eighth note
quarter rest	half note

Page 27, No. 6

Page 27, No. 7

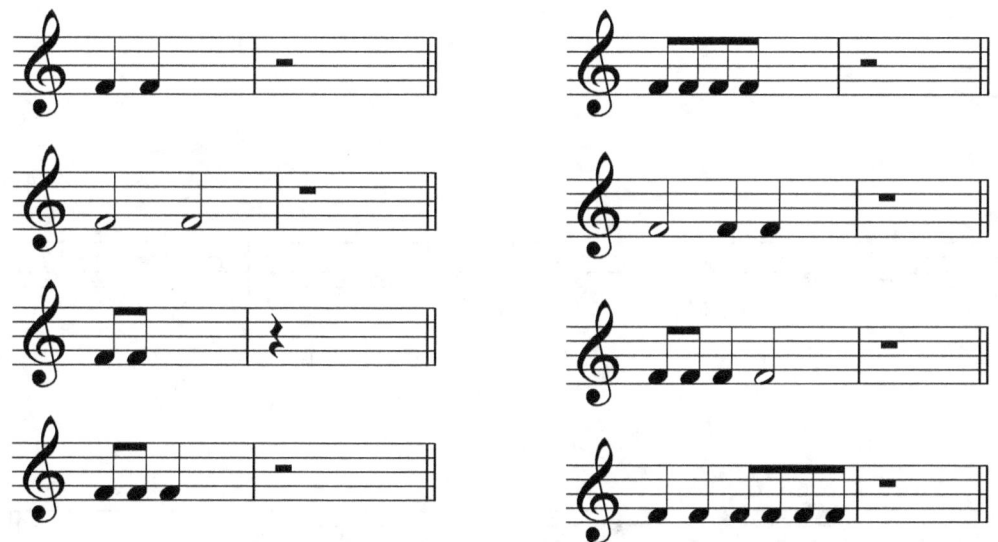

Page 29, No. 1

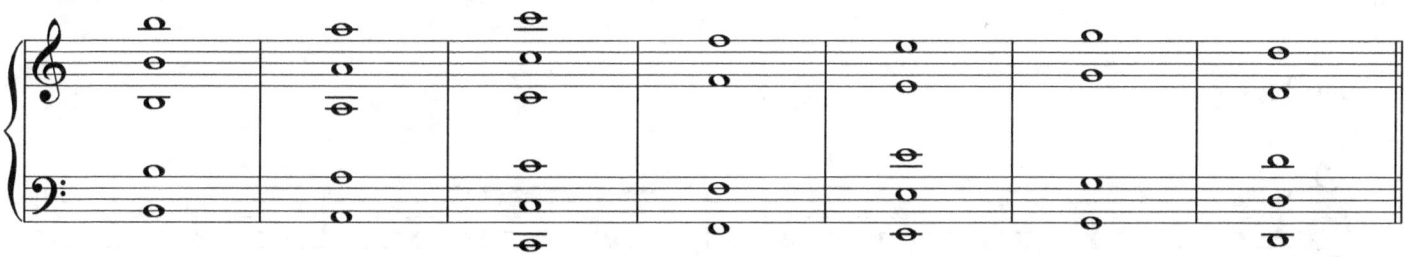

Page 29, No. 2

F E A D   C   G A   B G
4 1 2 1/2 1/2 1 1/2 2 1/2

©San Marco Publications 2022   4   Level 1

Page 29, No. 3

Page 30, No. 4

p	piano	soft
mp	mezzo piano	moderately soft
mf	mezzo forte	moderately loud
f	forte	loud

Page 30, No. 5

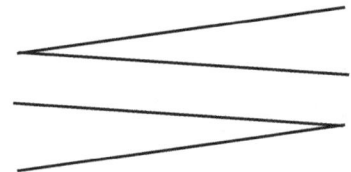

Page 33, No. 1

Page 34, No. 1

Page 34, No. 1, continued

Page 35, No. 2

2/4, 4/4, 2/4, 4/4, 3/4

Page 35, No. 3

Page 36, No. 4

Page 36, No. 5

Level 1

Page 38, No. 1

Page 41, No. 1, other answers are possible

Page 42, No. 2, other answers are possible

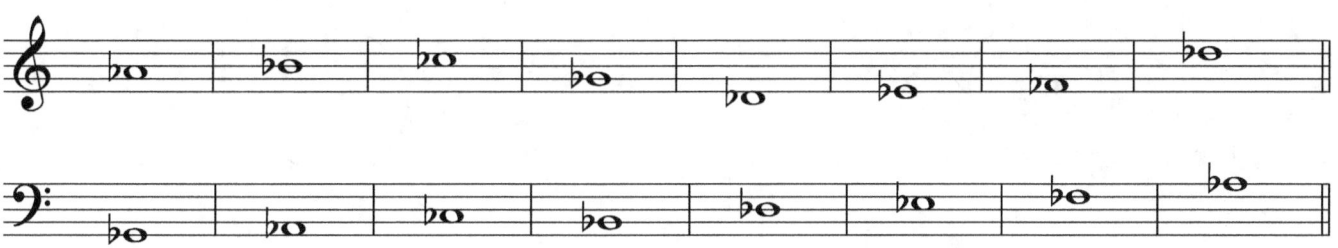

Page 44, No. 3

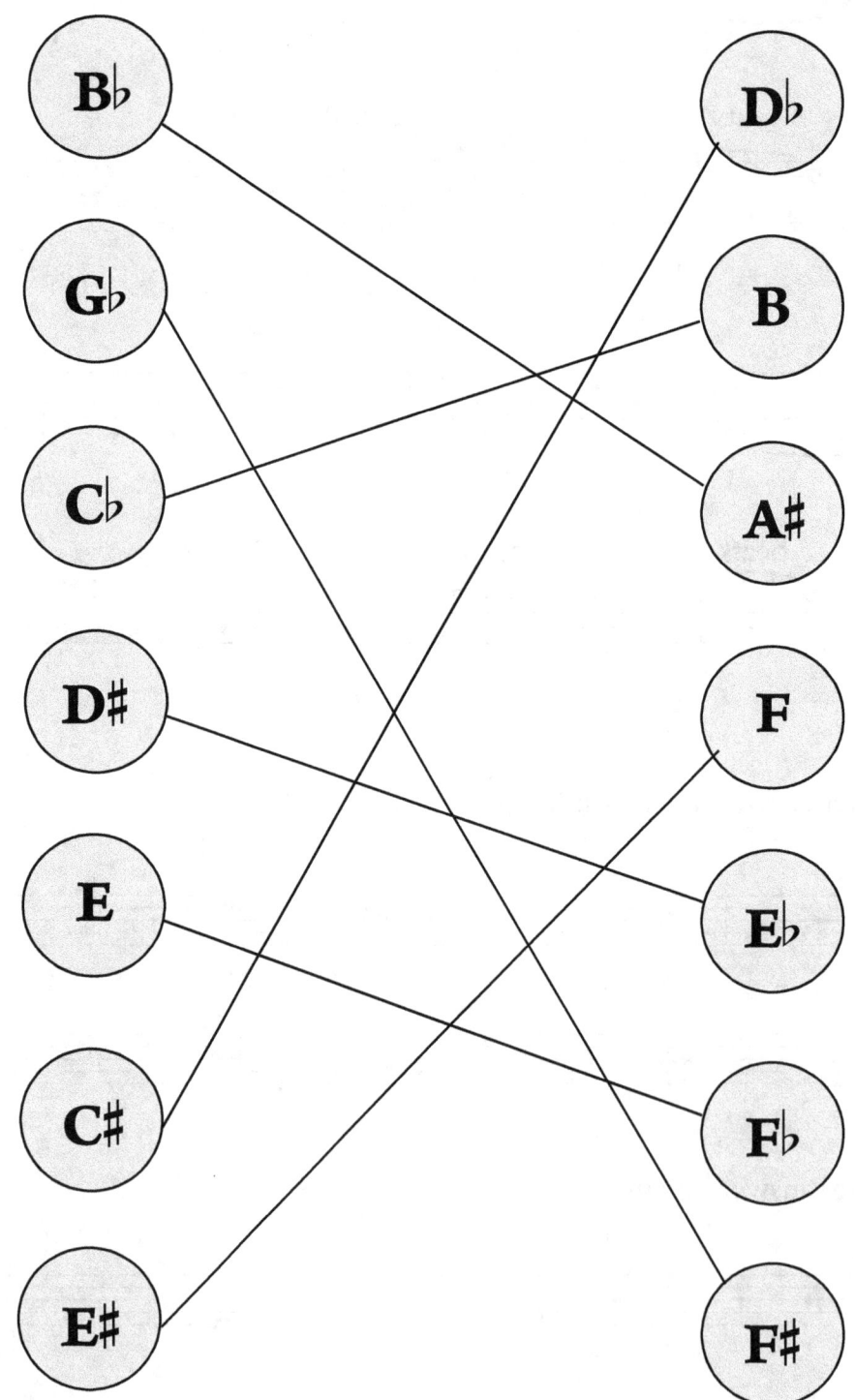

Level 1

Page 46, No. 1

F# E F# C# D A B♭ E♭ E F# E D

A♭ C E♭ A G# E G B B♭ D B♭ F#

Page 46, No. 2, other options are possible

Page 46, No. 3, other options are possible

Page 47, No. 4

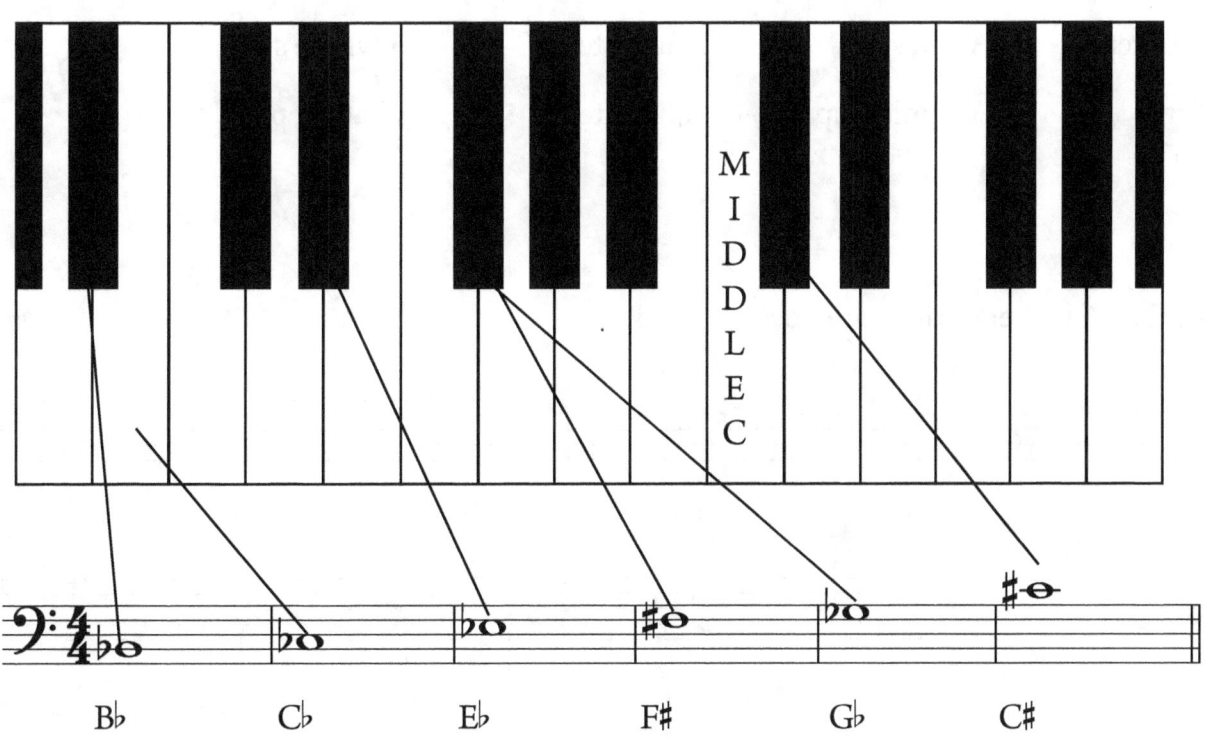

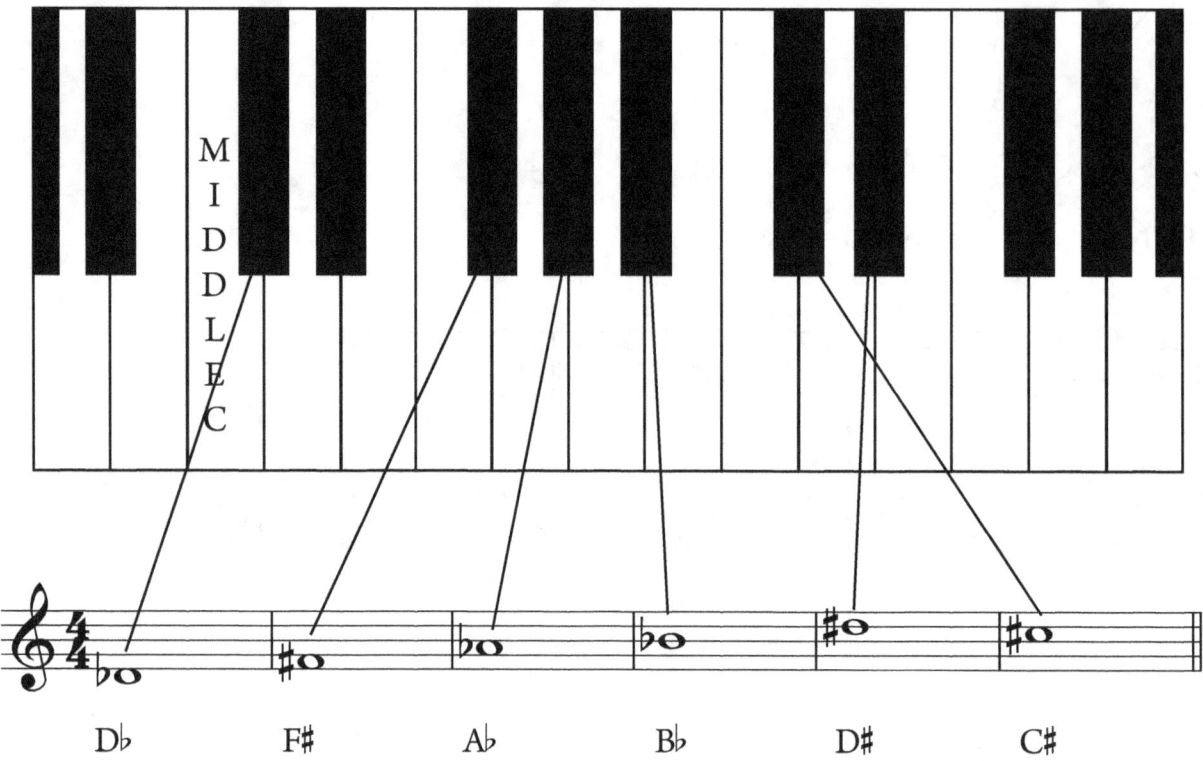

Page 48, No. 5

A whole step	A half step	A whole step	A whole step
A half step	A half step	A half step	A whole step
A whole step	A half step	A half step	A whole step
A half step	A whole step	A half step	A half step

Page 48, No. 6 (other options are possible)

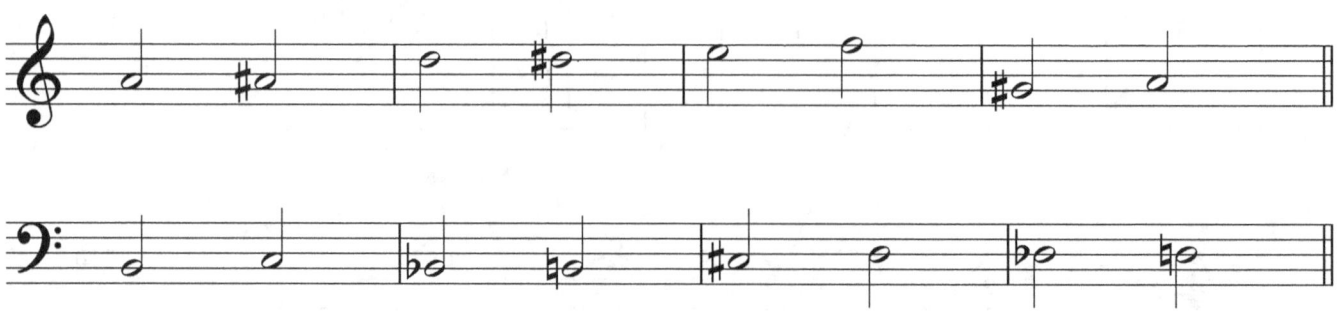

Page 49, No. 7 (other options are possible)

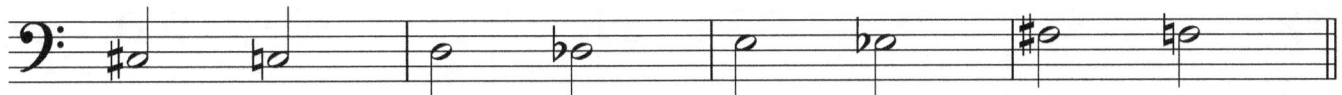

Page 49, No. 8

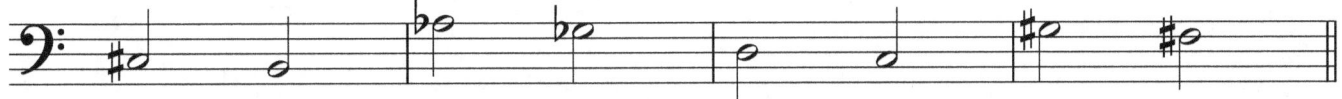

Page 49, No. 9

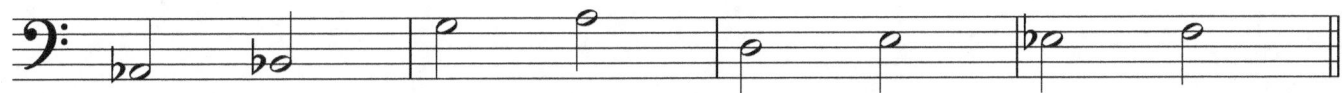

Page 51, No. 1

5 7 2 1 3 7 3 8

4 2 8 6 5 6 2 1

1 8 2 3 6 6 4 5

8 5 2 1 8 3 8 7

Page 52, No. 2

Page 53, No. 3

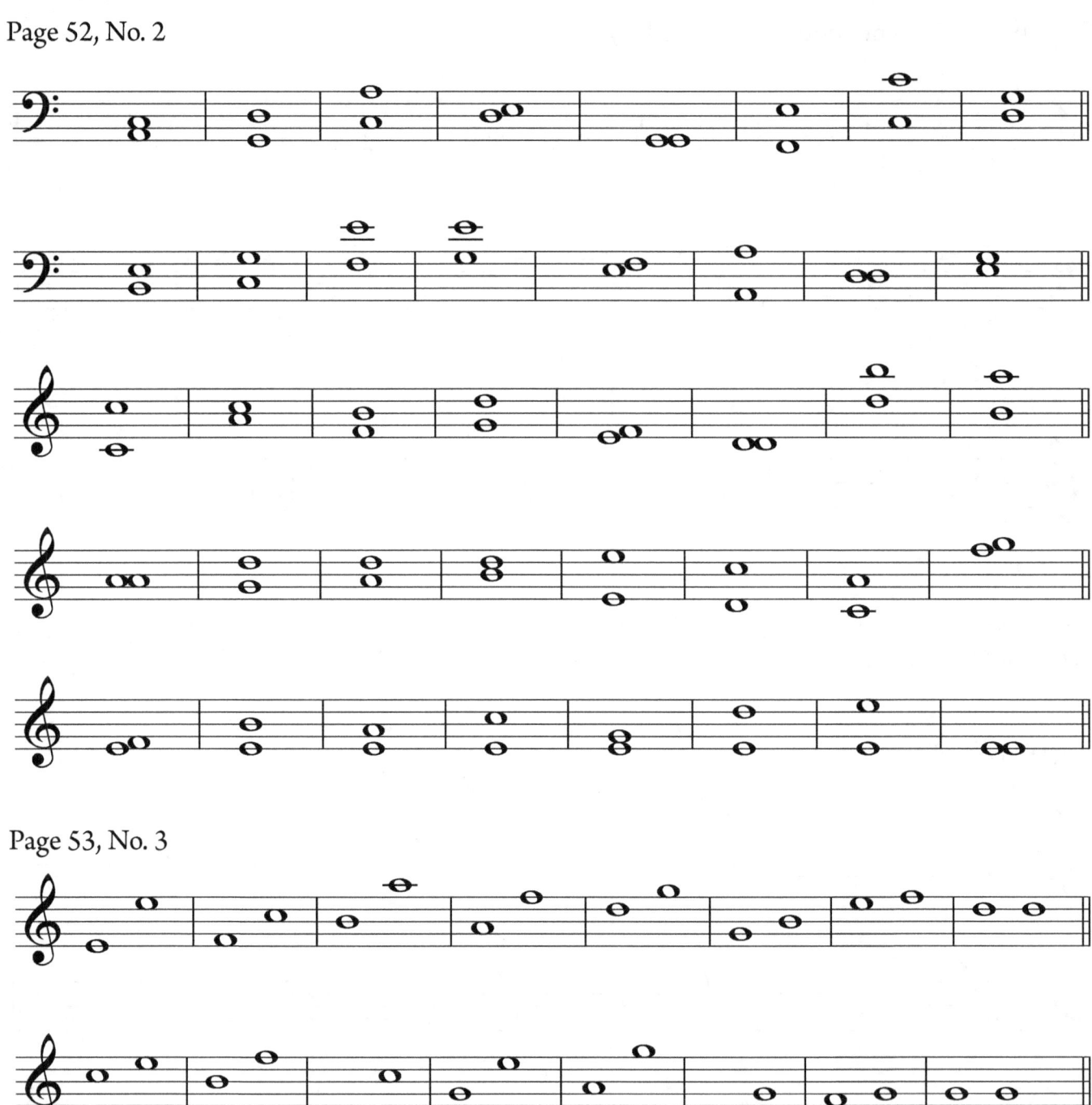

Page 58, No. 1

piano	soft
forte	loud
crescendo	becoming louder
mezzo forte	moderately loud
descrescendo	becoming softer
tie	curved line between two of the same notes meaning to hold for the combined value of both notes
accent	a stressed note
slur	curved line meaning to play the notes smoothly
mezzo piano	moderately soft
staccato	dot on a note meaning play the note short and detached
diminuendo	becoming softer

Page 59

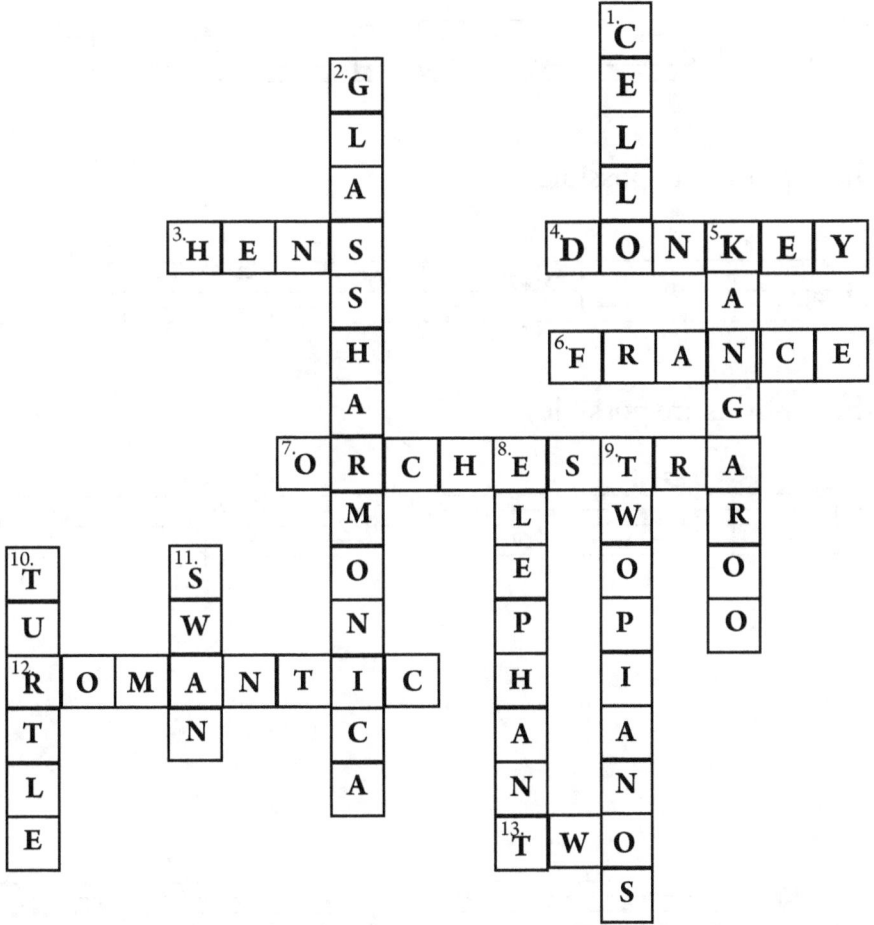

Page 60, No. 1 (Review)

4/4

2/4

Page 60, No. 2

Page 60, No. 3

Page 61, No. 4 (other options are possible)

Page 61, No. 5 (other options are possible)

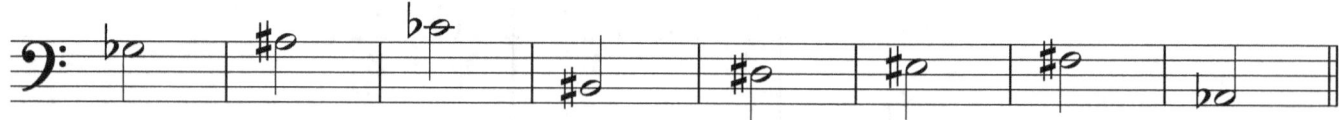

Page 61, No. 6

3 7 4 2 5 6 1 8

Page 61, No. 7

©San Marco Publications 2022   15   Level 1

Page 62, No. 8

a. ☑Conductor
b. ☑Maracas
c. ☑French Horn
d. ☑France
e. ☑3
f. ☑2 pianos
g. ☑Wolf
h. ☑Glass Harmonic
i. ☑Cello
j. ☑Program Music

Page 64, No. 1

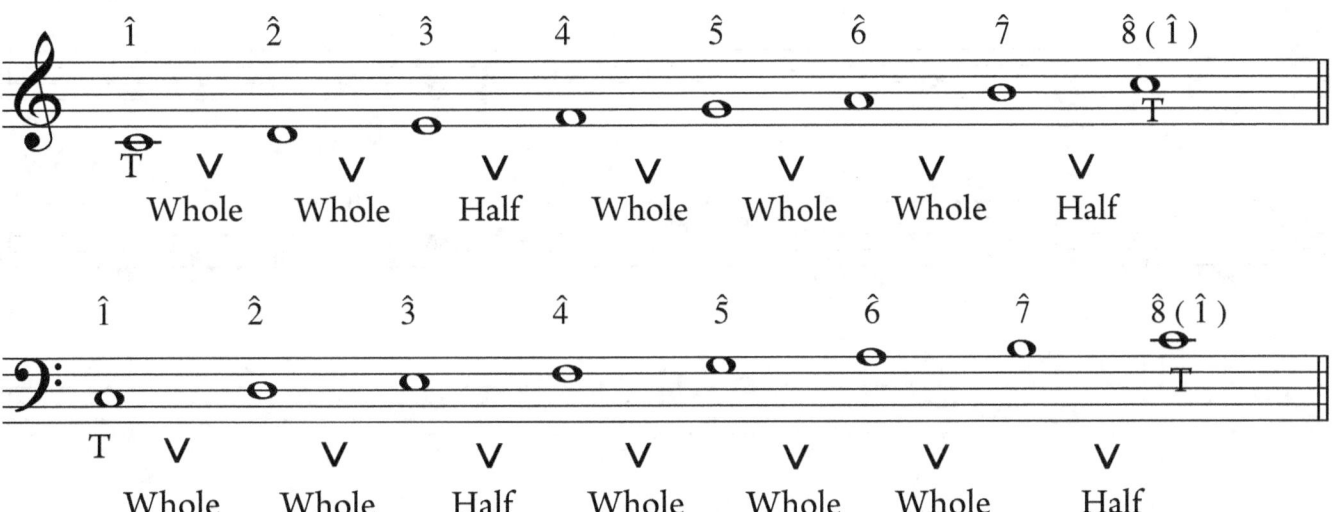

Page 65, No. 2

Page 65, No. 3

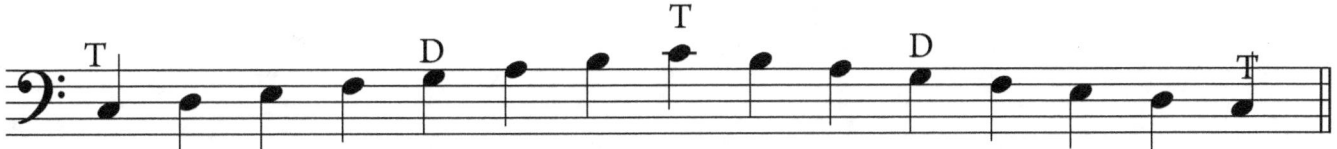

Page 66, No. 4

Page 67, No. 5

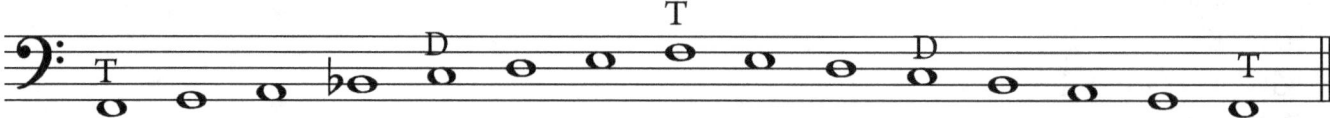

Page 68, No. 6

Page 69, No. 7

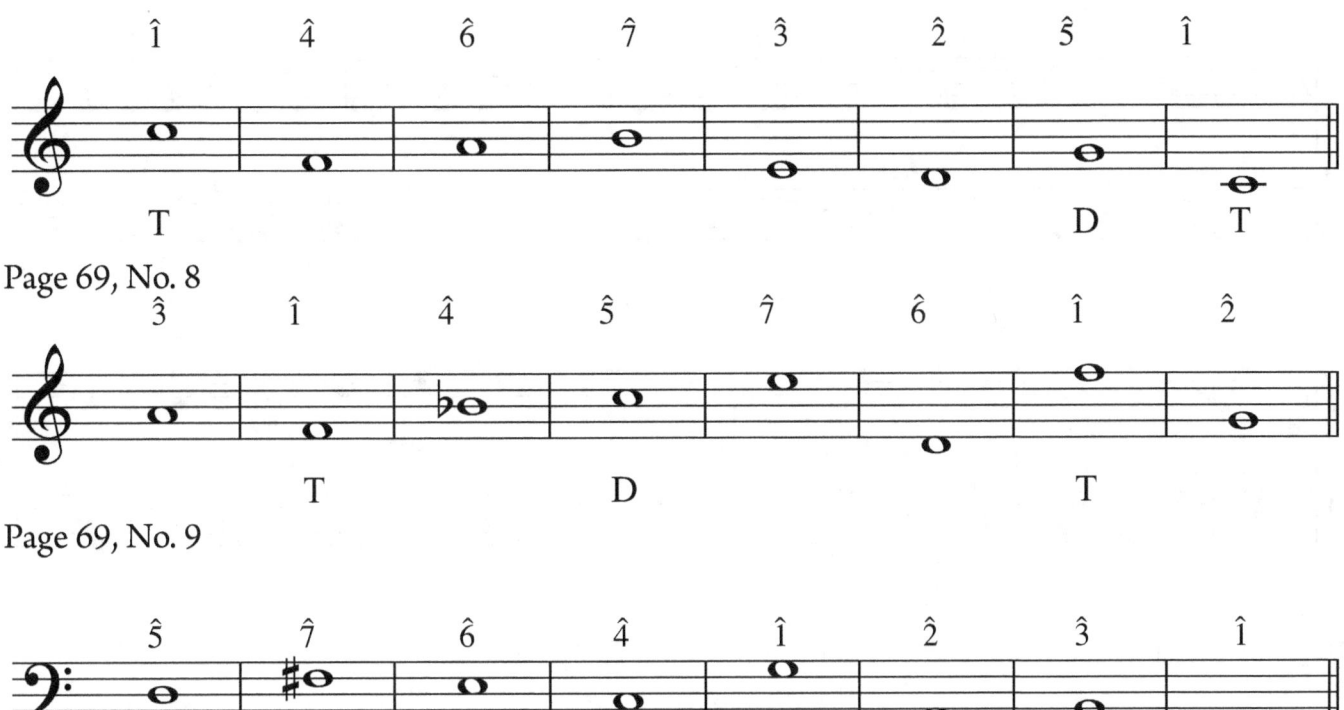

Page 69, No. 8

Page 69, No. 9

Page 71, No. 1

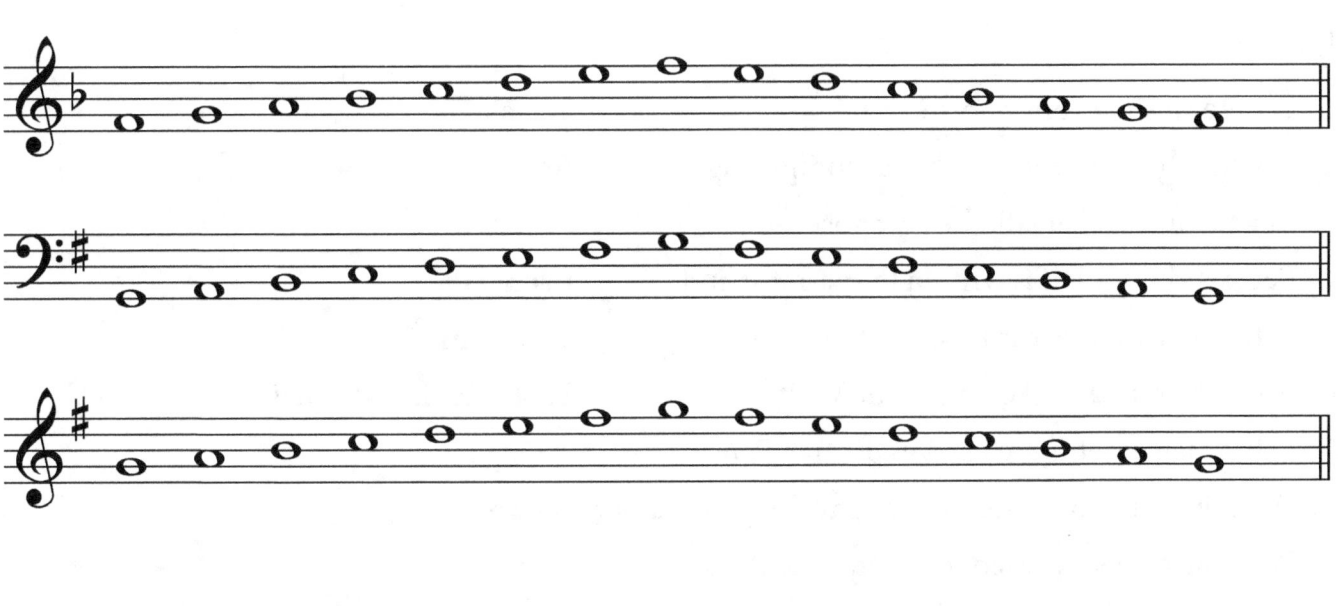

Page 72, No. 1

Page 73, No. 1

F major
G major
C major
F major

Page 77

1. Where was Prokofiev born? **Russia**
2. At what age did Prokofiev begin composing? **five**
3. In what musical era did he compose? **Modern**
4. Peter and the Wolf is written for narrator and **orchestra**
5. What type of music is Peter and the Wolf? **Program**
6. Name 4 animals in Peter and the Wolf. **Wolf, duck, cat, bird**
7. What instruments are used to portray Peter? **strings**
8. What instrument is used to portray the grandfather? **bassooon**
9. What instument is used to portray the duck? **oboe**

Page 78, No. 1

k) tempo
i) crescendo
e) moderato
c) piano
g) forte
j) andante
l) ritardando
f) mezzo piano
h) allegro
d) diminuendo
b) lento
a) mezzo forte

a) moderately loud
b) slow
c) soft
d) becoming softer
e) a moderate tempo
f) moderately soft
g) loud
h) fast
i) becoming louder
j) moderately slow; walking pace
k) speed at which music is performed
l) slowing down gradually

Page 80, No. 1

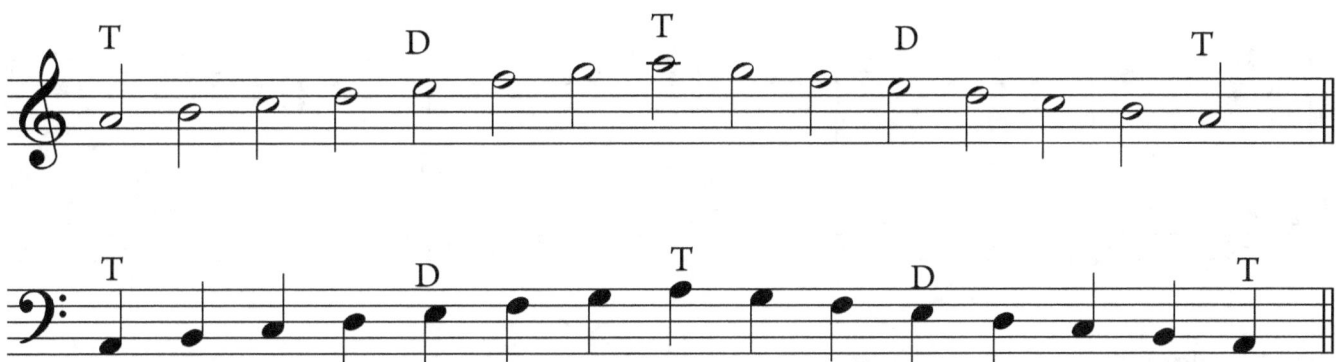

Page 83, No. 1

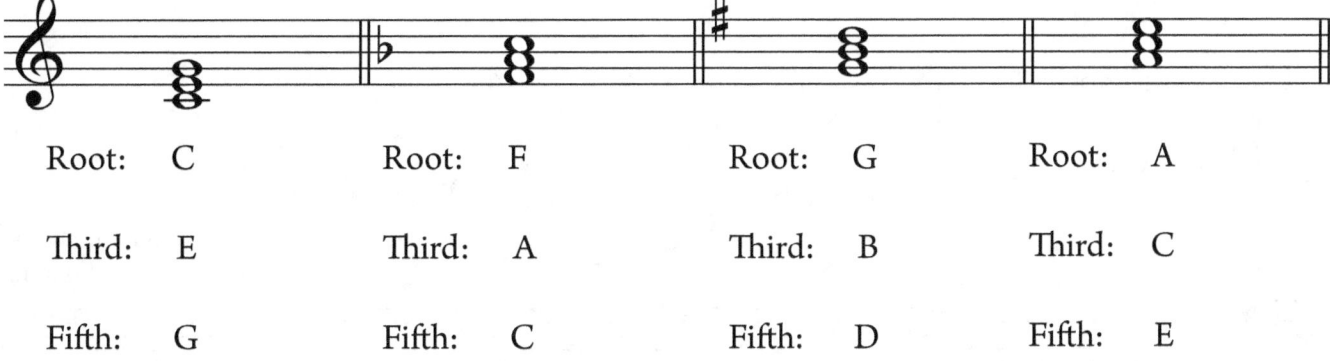

Root: C Root: F Root: G Root: A

Third: E Third: A Third: B Third: C

Fifth: G Fifth: C Fifth: D Fifth: E

Page 84, No. 2

F major	G major	C major	C major
F major	G major	G major	F major
A minor	C major	F major	G major
A minor	G major	F major	C major

Page 84, No. 3

Page 85, No. 4

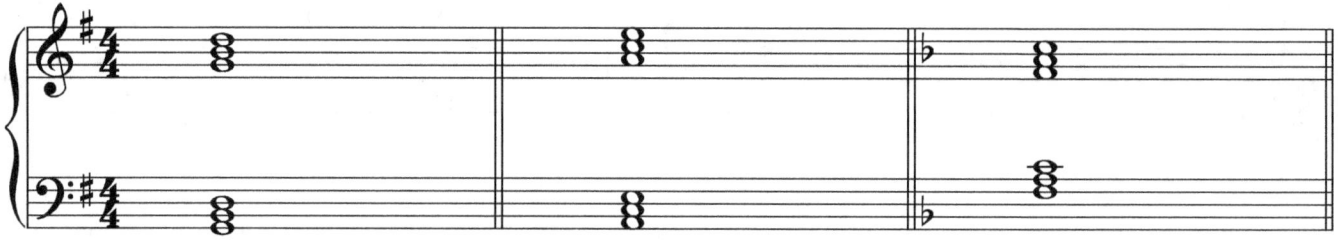

Page 85, No. 5

Triad	Root	3rd	5th
F major	F	A	C
G major	G	B	D
C major	C	E	G
A minor	A	C	E

Page 85, No. 6

Antonin Dvorak
Sonatina

key: G major

Wolfgang Amadeus Mozart
Dissonant Quartet

key: C major

Johann Sebastian Bach
Invention No. 8

key: F major

Page 87, No.1

English Folk Song

key: F major

Norwegian Folk Song

key: C major

Page 89, No.1 (other options are possible)

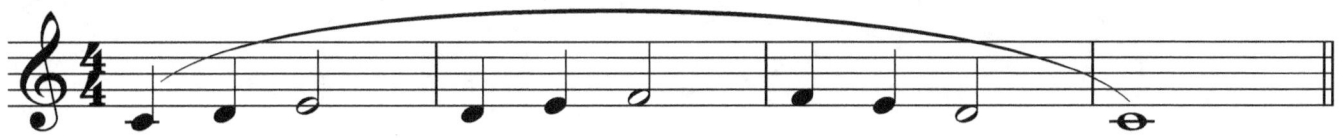

Page 89, No. 2 (other options are possible)

Page 89, No.3

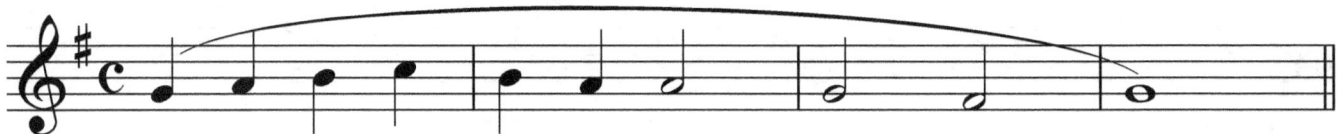

Page 90, No. 1

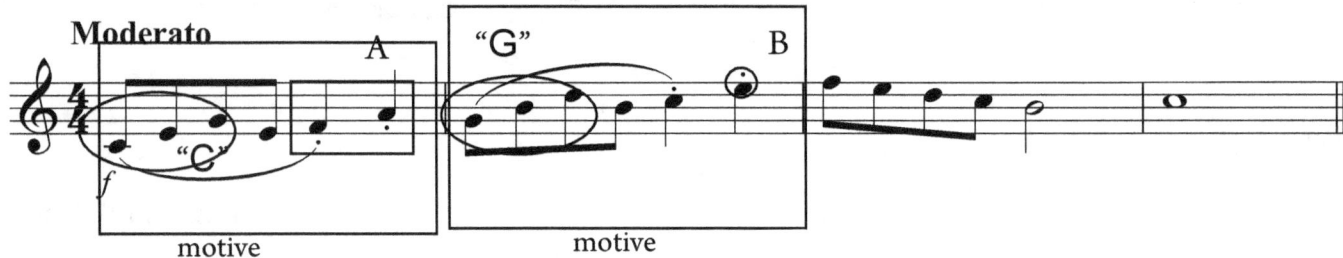

a. Add the correct time signature directly on the music.

b. Name the key of this piece. C major

c. Name the interval at A. 3rd

d. Find and circle a C major triad. Label it "C."

e. Find and circle a G major triad. Label it "G."

f. Define **Moderato**. at a moderate speed

g. Name and define the sign at letter B. staccato, play short and detached

h. Find a motive and draw a square around each time it occurs.

i. How many slurs are in this piece?   2

Page 91

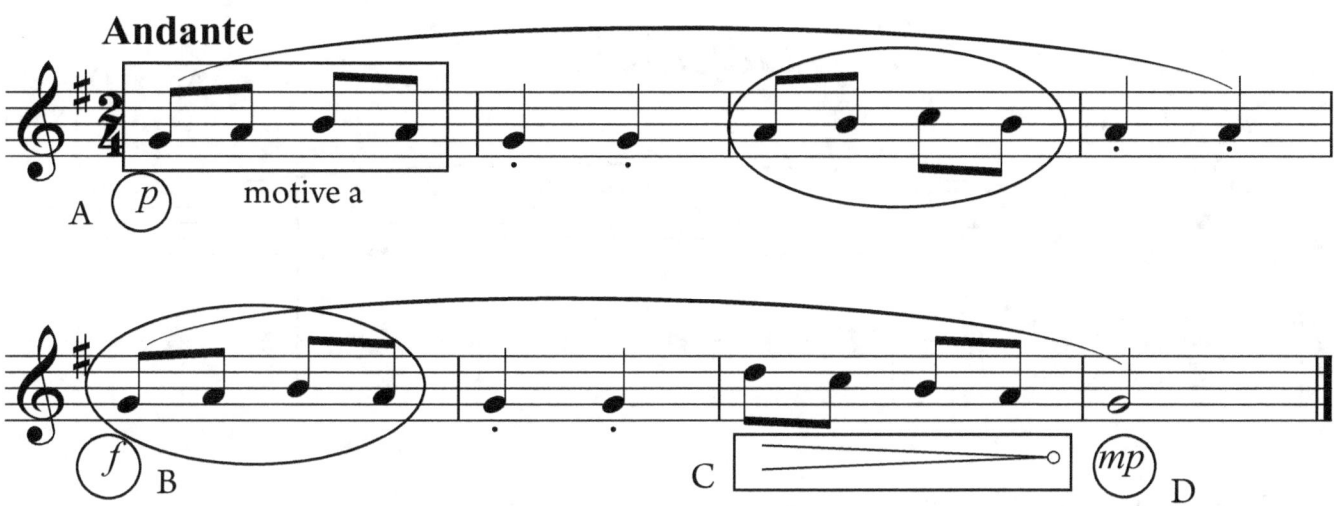

a. Add the correct time signature directly on the music.

b. Name the key of this piece. G major

c. Circle each time motive "a" appears in this piece.

d. How many phrases are in this piece? 2.

e. On which scale degree does phrase two end? $\hat{1}$

f. Define **Andante**. moderately slow, at a walking pace

g. Name and define the sign at letter A. piano, play soft

h. Name and define the sign at letter B. forte, play loud

i. Name and define the sign at letter C. decrescendo, becoming softer

j. Name and define the sign at letter D. mezzo piano, play moderately soft

Page 92

Bagatelle

Anton Diabelli
(1781 - 1858)

a. What is the title of this piece? Bagatelle

b. Who is the composer? Anton Diabelli

c. Name the key of this piece G major

d. Add the time signature directly on the music.

e. How many phrases are in this piece? 1.

f. On which scale degree does the melody this piece begin? $\hat{5}$

g. Define *Allegro*. fast

h. Name the interval at A. 3rd

i. Name the interval at B. 4th

j. This piece is played:

☑loud ☐soft

©San Marco Publications 2022   25   Level 1

Page 93, No. 1

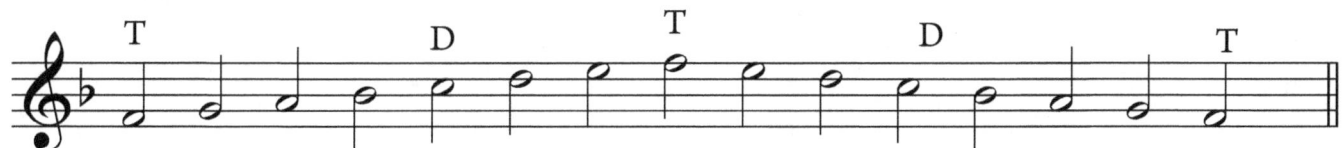

Page 93, No. 2

Page 93, No. 3

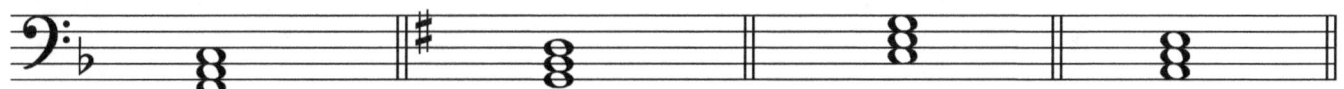

Page 94, No. 4

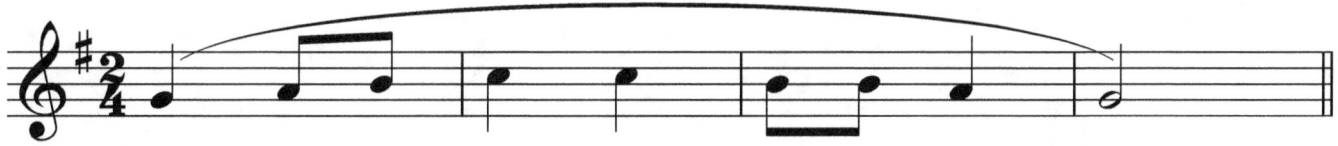

Page 94, No. 5

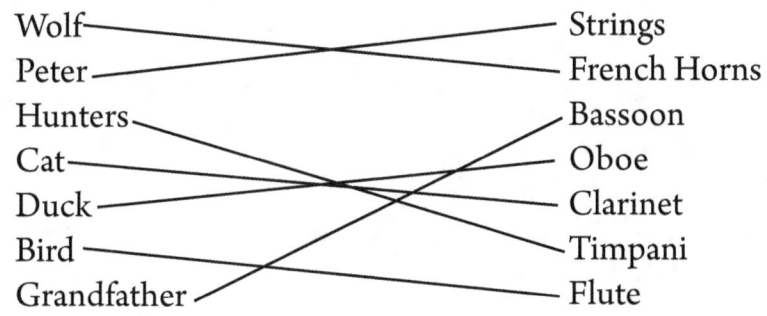

Page 95, No. 6

a. F
b. F
c. T
d. T
e. F
f. T
g. T

Page 95, No. 7

a. rit
b. dim
c. cresc
d. decresc
e. mp
f. ff

Level 2

Page 3, No. 1

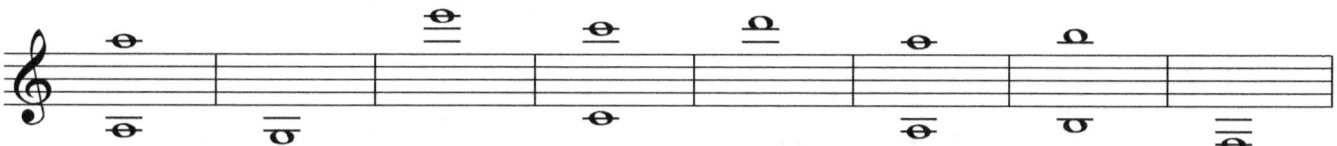

Page 3, No. 2

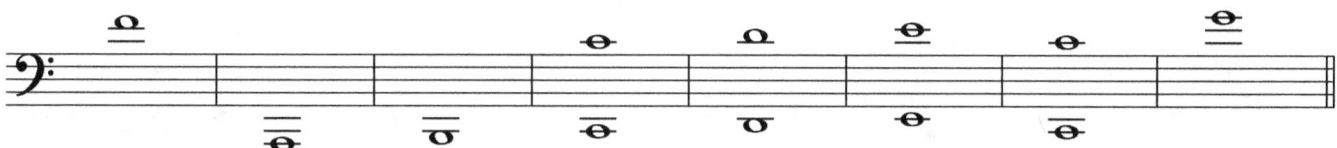

Page 3, No. 3

A C♯ G B♭ D E B A

B C♯ D♭ B F G F G

Page 3, No. 4

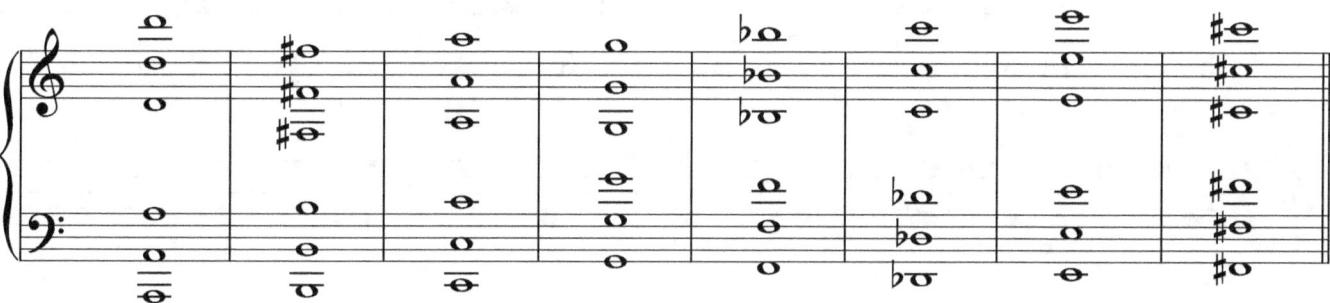

Page 4, No. 1

Page 4, No. 2

Page 5, No. 1

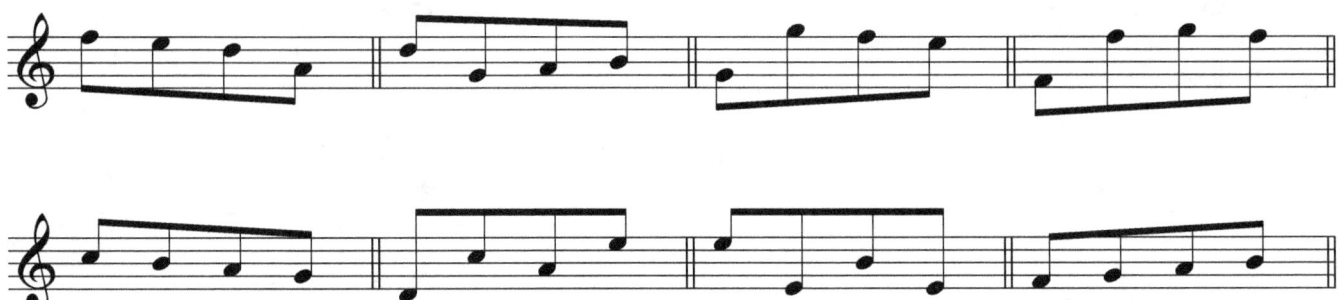

Page 8, No. 1

Page 8, No. 2

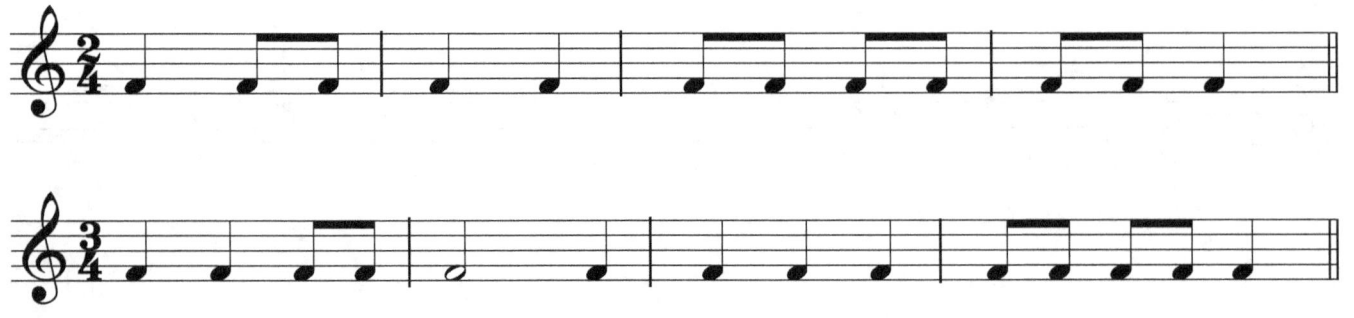

Page 10, No. 1

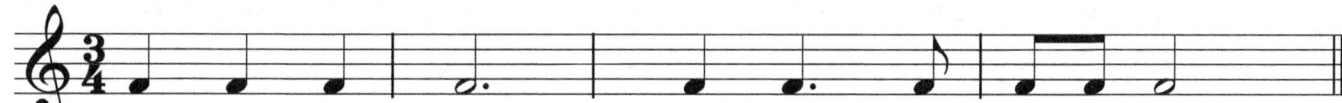

Page 11, No. 2

Page 12, No. 1

Page 12, No. 2

Page 16, No. 1

Page 16, No. 2

Page 17, No. 3

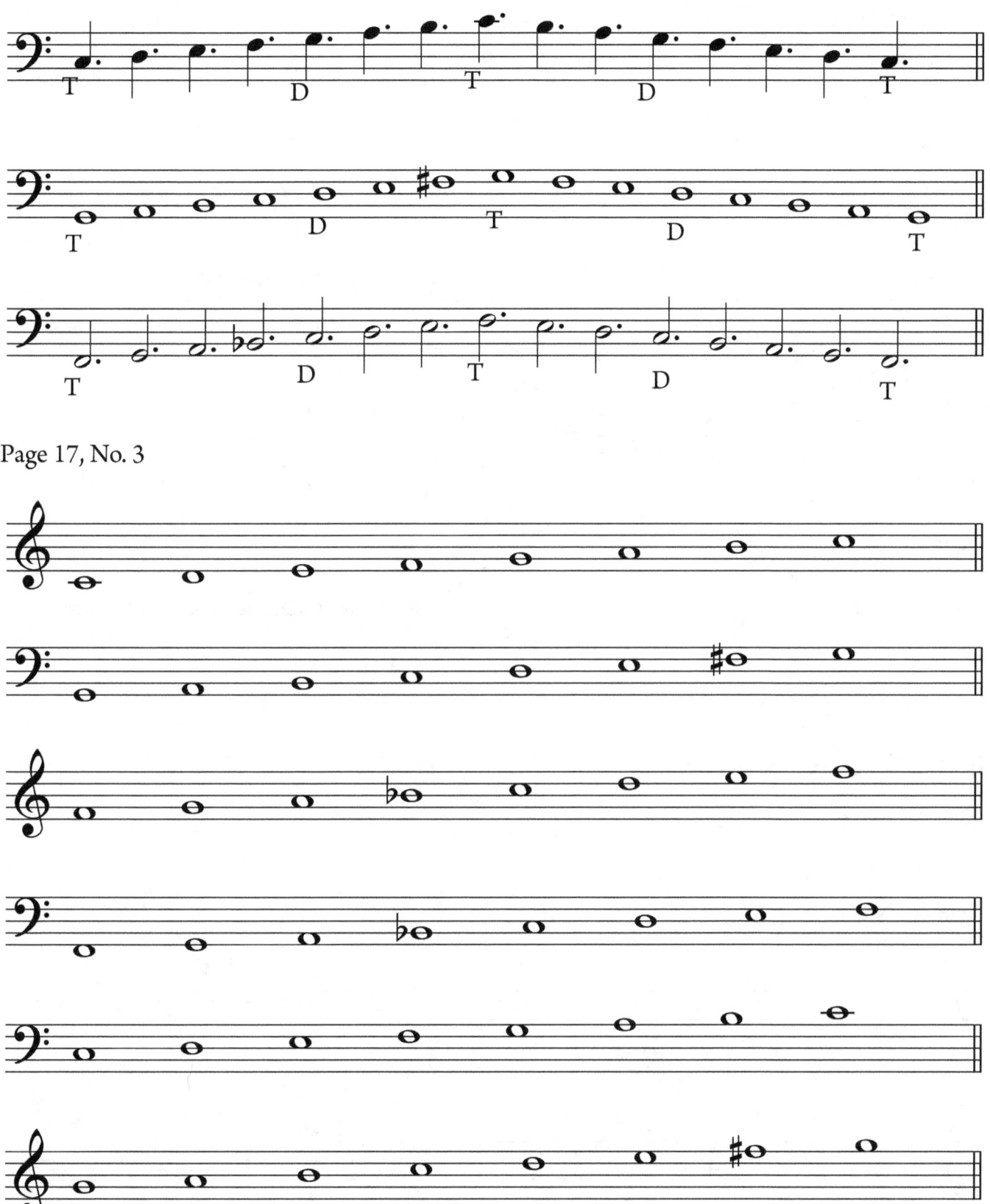

Page 18, No. 4

1 2 7 3 5 4
1 6 7 5 6
5 1 4 2 7
1 7 6 4 2

Page 19, No. 5

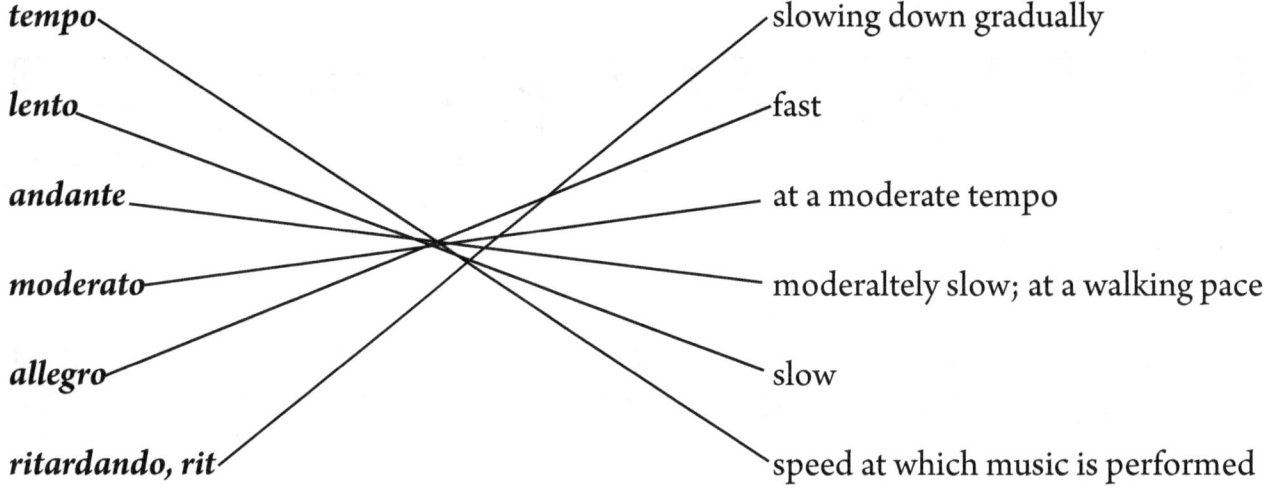

tempo — speed at which music is performed
lento — slow
andante — moderaltely slow; at a walking pace
moderato — at a moderate tempo
allegro — fast
ritardando, rit — slowing down gradually

Page 20, No. 1 (Review 1)

E B D A C B G F
C D D E E G B A

Page 20, No. 2

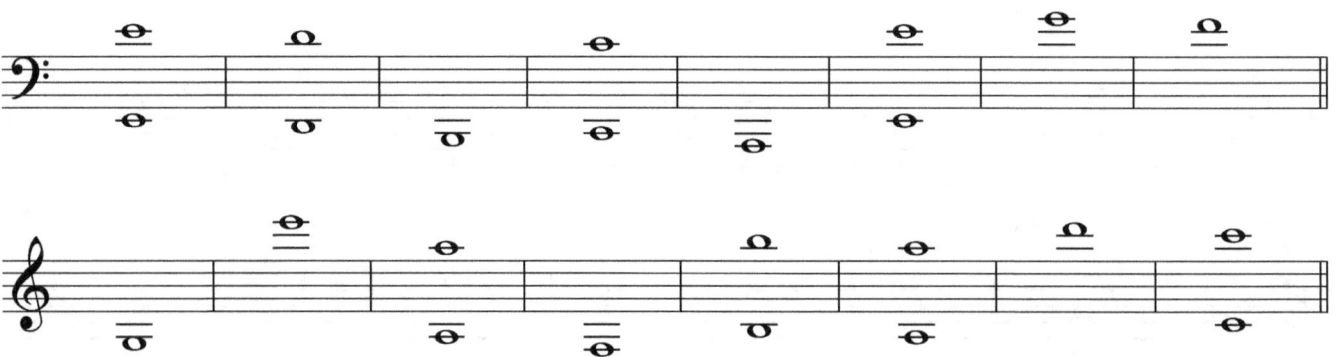

Page 21, No. 3

Page 21, No. 4

Page 22, No. 5

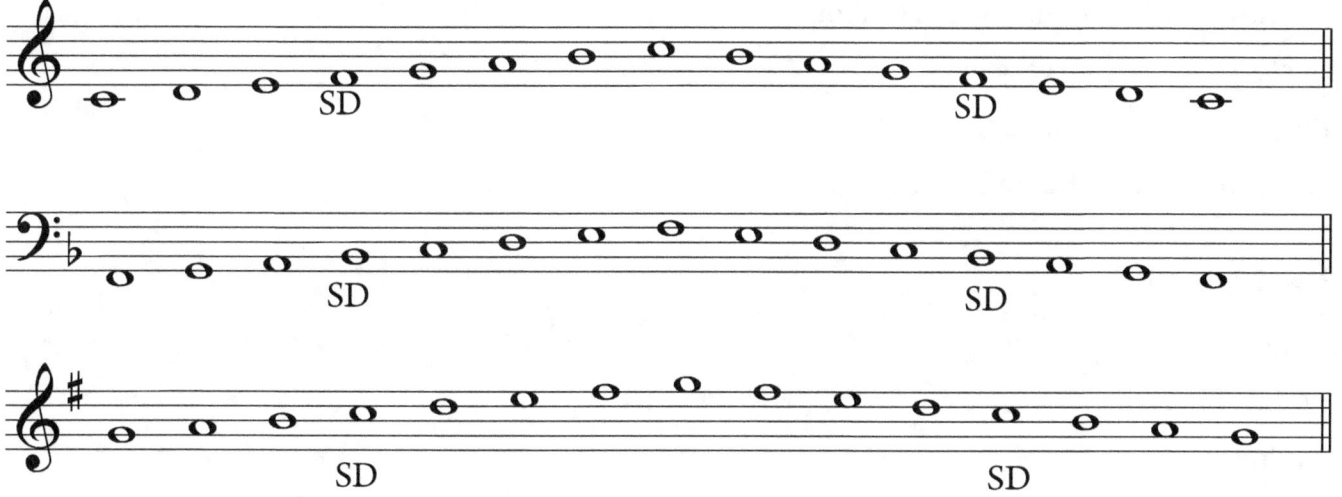

Page 22, No. 6

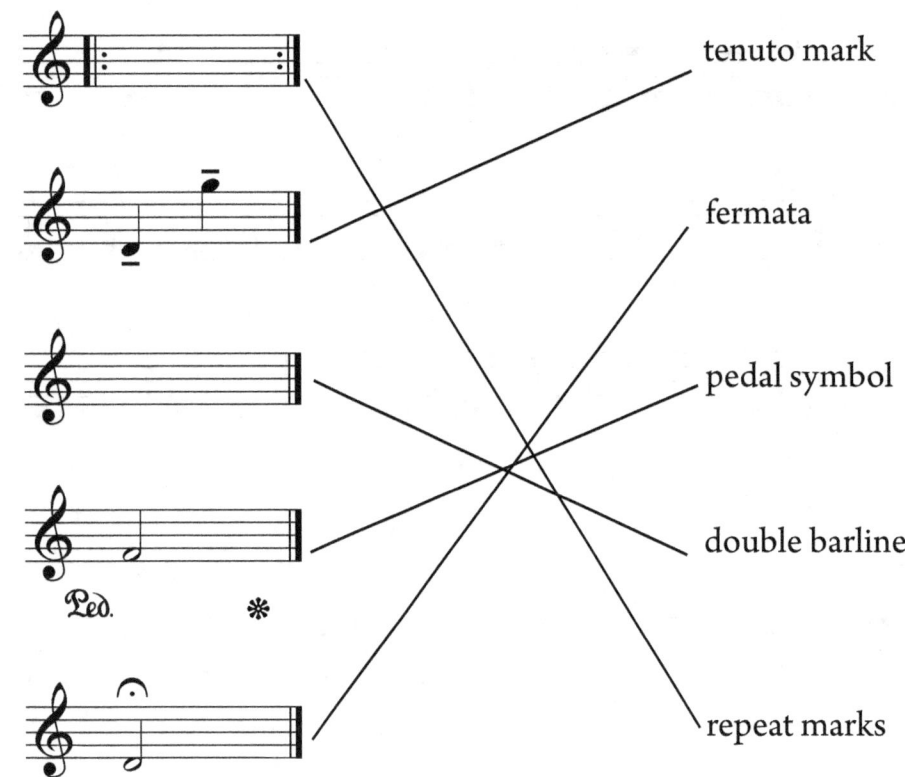

Page 23, No. 7

tempo	speed at which music is performed
lento	slow
moderato	at a moderate tempo
rallentando, rall.	slowing down
a tempo	return to the original tempo
allegretto	fairly fast, not as fast as allegro
andante	moderate, walking pace
presto	very fast
allegro	fast
ritardando, rit	slowing down gradually

Page 27, No. 1

A minor

E minor

D minor

Page 27, No. 2

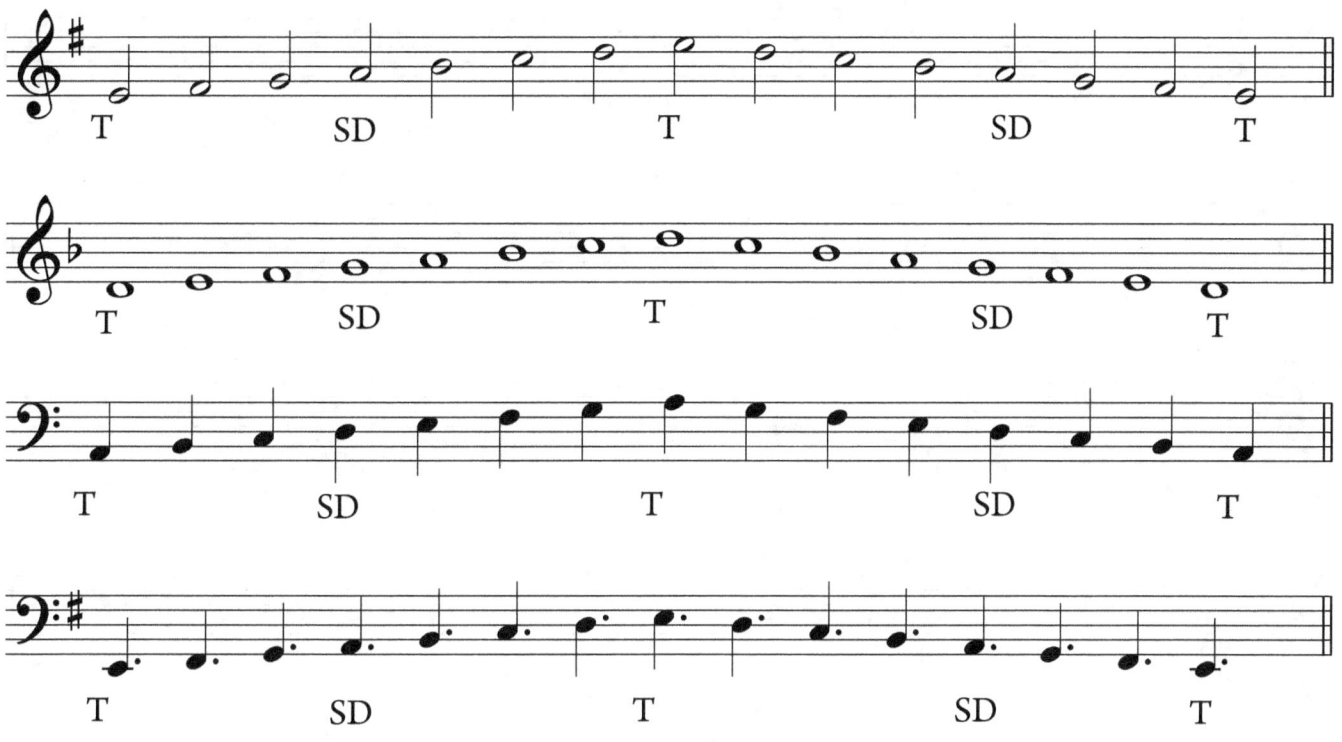

Page 29, No. 1

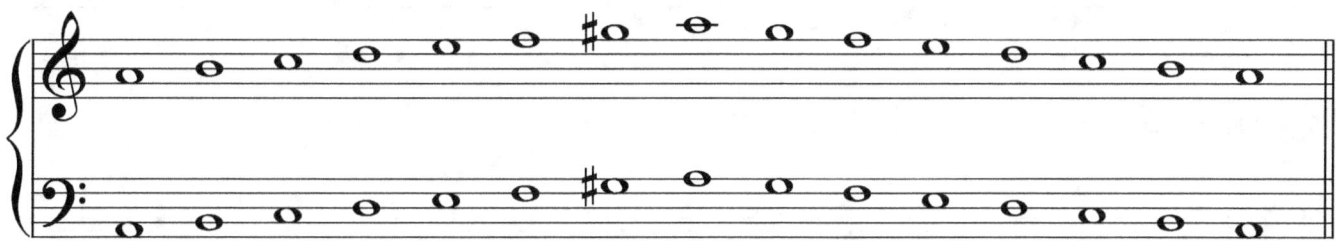

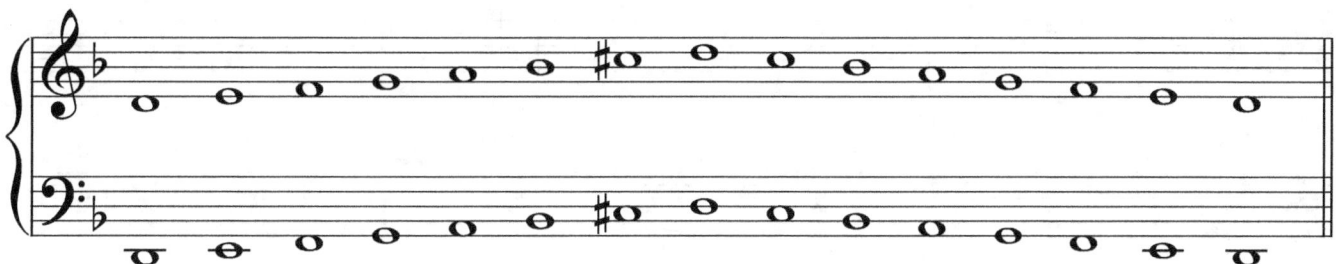

Page 30, No. 2

Page 31, No. 3

Page 33, No. 1

Page 33, No. 2

Page 34, No. 1

Page 34, No. 2

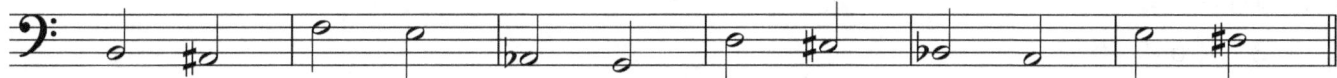

Page 35, No. 1

Page 35, No. 2

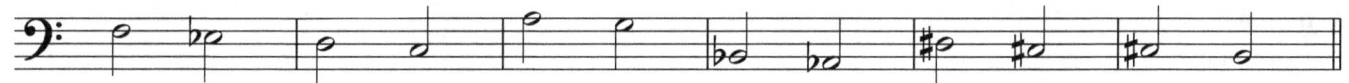

Page 36, No. 1

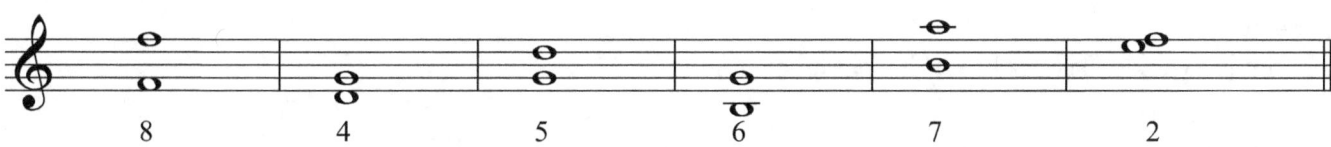

© San Marco Publications 2022   Level 2

Page 36, No. 2

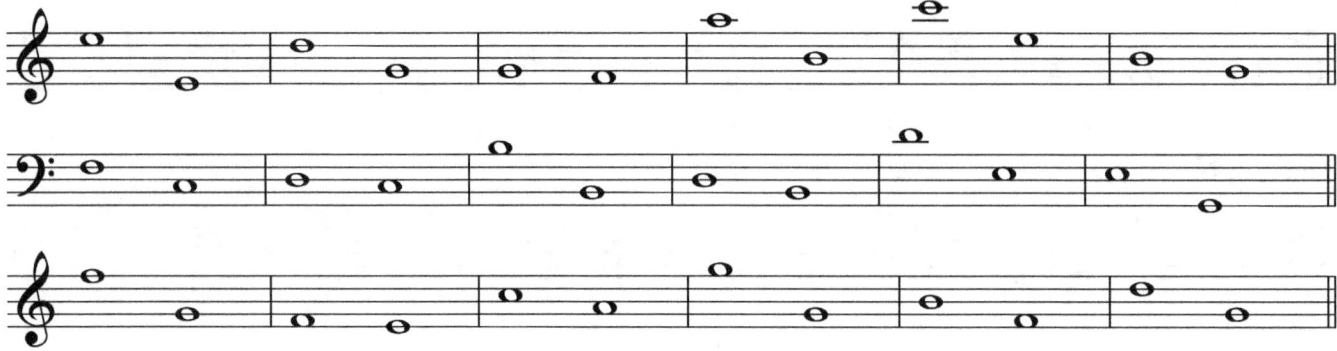

Page 37, No. 3

4 5 3 8 6 7 6 2

7 5 3 2 1 4 5 6

2 4 8 3 1 8 5 5

8 2 5 1 3 7 4 4

Page 40, No. 1

a. Austria
b. His father
c. classical
d. french horn
e. movements
f. rondo
g. piano
h. 12
i. theme
j. Twinkle Twinkle, Baa Baa Black Sheep, Alphabet Song

Page 44, No. 1

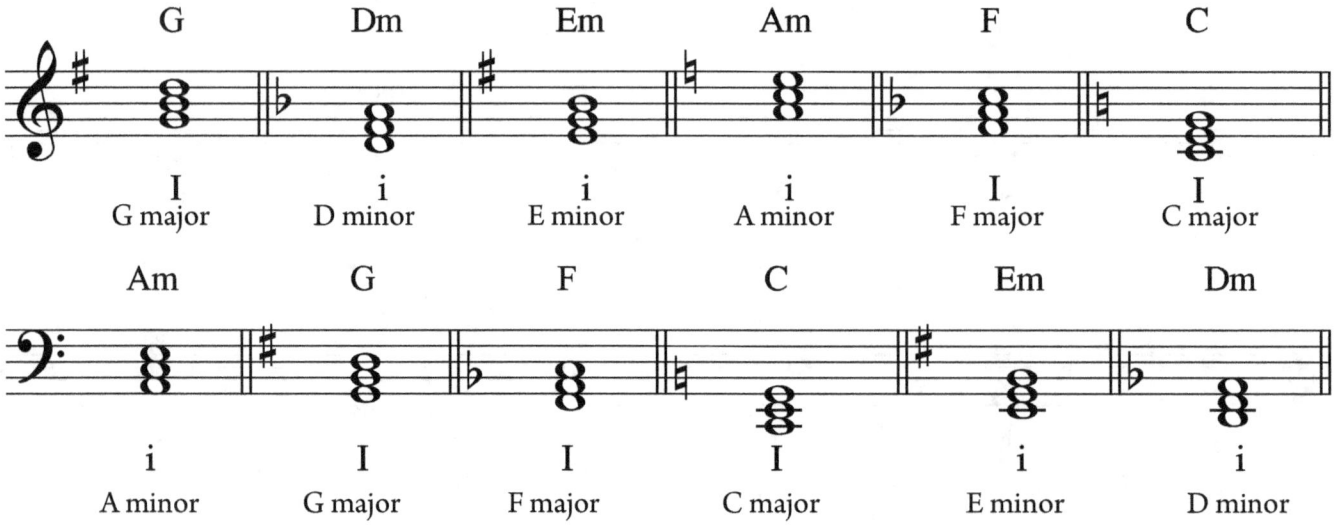

© San Marco Publications 2022

Page 44, No. 2 (naturals are optional, but not necessary after double bar)

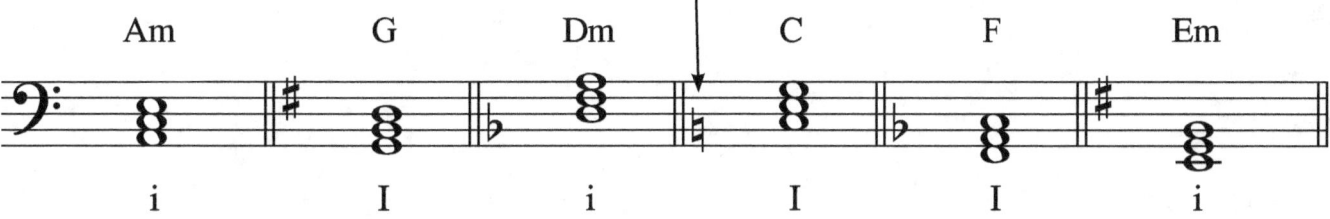

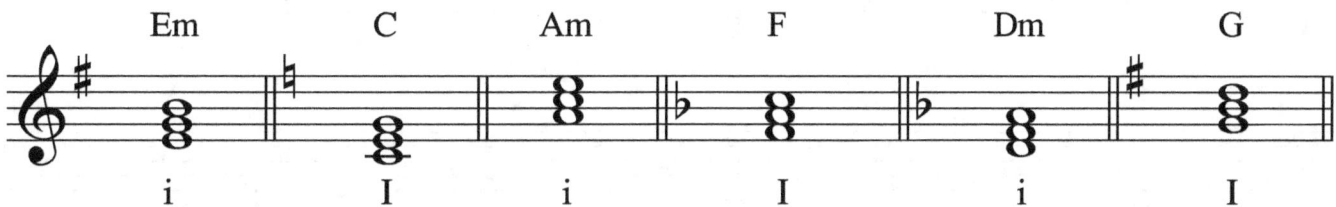

Page 45, No. 3

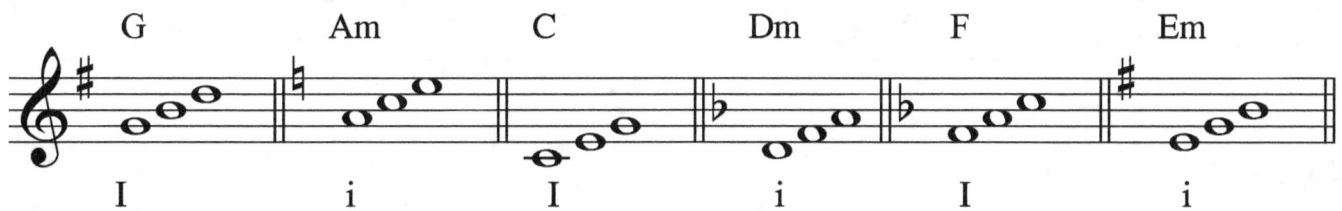

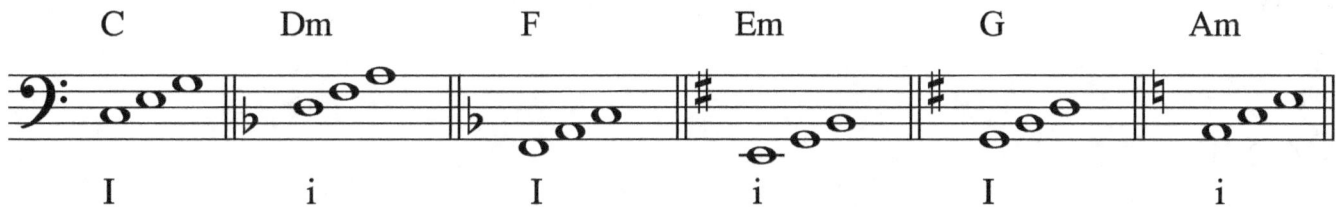

Page 45, No. 4

chord symbol:	**C**	chord symbol:	**Dm**	chord symbol:	**G**
key:	**C major**	key:	**D minor**	key:	**G major**
root:	**C**	root:	**D**	root:	**G**
3rd:	**E**	3rd:	**F**	3rd:	**B**
5th:	**G**	5th:	**A**	5th:	**D**
chord symbol:	**Em**	chord symbol:	**Am**	chord symbol:	**F**
key:	**E minor**	key:	**A minor**	key:	**F major**
root:	**E**	root:	**A**	root:	**F**
3rd:	**G**	3rd:	**C**	3rd:	**A**
5th:	**B**	5th:	**E**	5th:	**C**

© San Marco Publications 2022

Page 47, No. 1 (Review 2)

C major
F major
G major

Page 47, No. 2

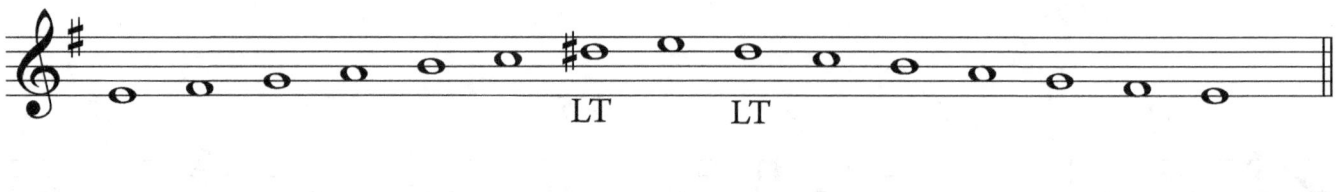

Page 48, No. 3

H H H W W H
W W H H W W

Page 48, No. 4

5 6 2 1 3 8 7 4
8 4 1 6 5 7 3 6
1 3 2 8 7 6 4 5

Page 49, No. 5

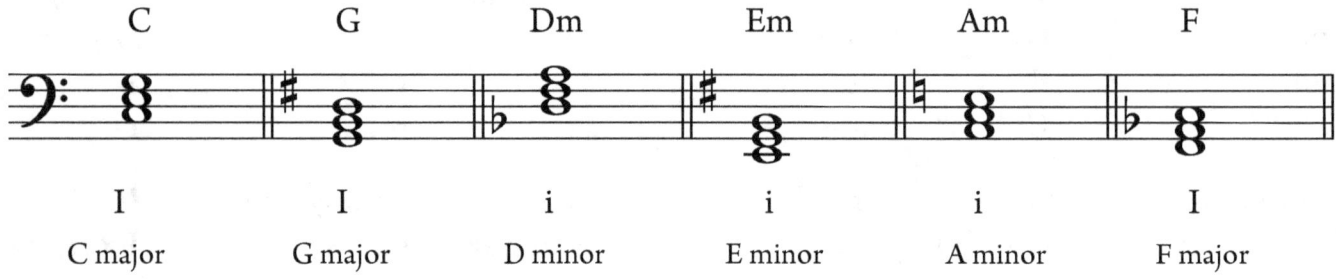

Page 49, No. 6

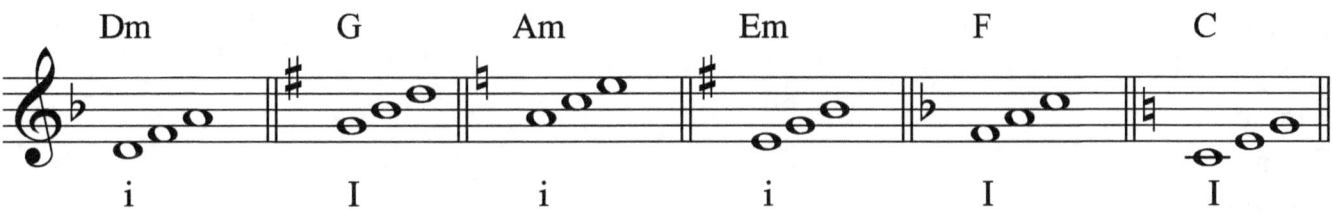

Page 49, No. 7

poco — little

molto — much very

fine — the end

da capo, D.C. — from the beginning

D.C. al fine — repeat from the beginning and end at fine

Page 50, No. 8

a. In what country was Mozart born? **Austria**

b. Name one instrument Mozart played. **piano, violin**

c. How old was Mozart when he wrote his first opera?

☐ 5   ☑ 12   ☐ 7

d. Who was Mozart's first teacher? **His father**

e. What is the solo instrument in Mozarts horn concerto? **French horn**

f. For which instument are the variations "Ah vous dirai-je, Maman" written? **Piano**

g. How many variations are there in "Ah vous dirai-je, Maman?" **Twelve**

h. Name one popular childrens song based on this theme. **Twinkle, Twinkle Baa Baa Black Sheep, Alphabet Song**

Page 53, No. 1

G major
F major
A minor
C major
E minor
D minor
G major

Page 54

1. Fairly fast, slower than allegro — allegretto
2. Very loud — fortissimo
3. Little — poco
4. Much, very — molto
5. The end — fine
6. Very fast — presto
7. Very soft — pianissimo
8. At a moderate tempo — moderato
9. Soft — piano
10. Moderately loud — mezzo piano
11. Loud — forte
12. Becoming louder — crescendo
13. Play smoothly — legato
14. Play short and detached — staccato

Page 56, No. 1

F major	$\hat{2}$	unstable
C major	$\hat{1}$	stable
G major	$\hat{3}$	stable

© San Marco Publications 2022 — Level 2

Page 57, No. 1

F major

C major

G major

Page 59, No. 1 (other options are possible)

Page 59, No. 2 (other options are possible)

Page 59, No. 3 (other options are possible)

© San Marco Publications 2022   Level 2

Page 60, No. 4 (other options are possible)

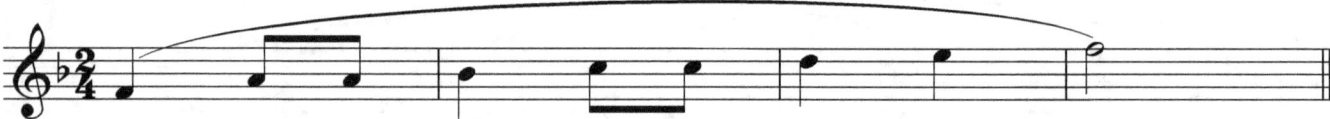

Page 60, No. 5 (other options are possible)

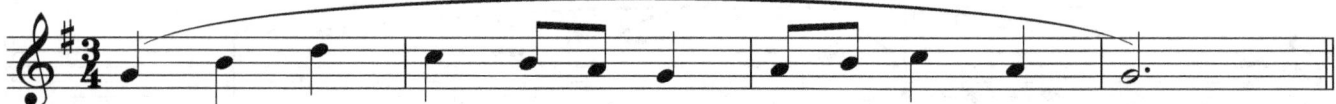

Page 60, No. 6

Page 61, No. 1

a. Add the correct time signature directly on the music.

b. Name the key of this piece. **F major**

c. Circle a complete F major scale in this piece.

d. Draw a phrase mark over the phrase.

e. On which scale degree does this phrase end? **$\hat{1}$**

f. Is this a stable degree? **yes**

g. Define *Allegro*. **fast**

h. Explain the sign at letter A. **fortissimo, very loud**

i. Explain the sign at letter B. **fermata, pause**

j. Label all the leading tones **LT.**

Page 62

a. Add the correct time signature directly on the music.

b. Name the key of this piece. **G major**

c. Circle each time motive "a" appears in this piece.

d. There are two phrases. Draw a phrase mark over each phrase.

e. On which scale degree does this phrase one end? $\hat{2}$

f. Is this a stable degree? **no**

g. Define *Presto*. **very fast**

h. Explain the sign at letter A. **mezzo piano, moderately soft**

i. Explain the sign at letter B. **pianissimo, very soft**

j. Name and define the sign at letter C. **staccato, play short and detached**

Allegro in C

Alexander Reinagle
(1756 - 1809)

a. Give the title of this piece. **Allegro in C**

b. Add the correct time signature directly on the music.

c. Name the key of this piece. **C major**

d. Name the composer of this piece. **Alexander Reinagle**

e. When did he live? **1756- 1809**

f. There are two phrases. Draw a phrase mark over each phrase.

g. On which scale degree does phrase two end? **$\hat{1}$**

h. Is this a stable degree? **yes**

i. Define *Molto allegro*. **Very fast**

j. Name and define the sign at A. **forte, loud**

k. Name the interval at B. **3rd**

Page 64, No. 1 (Review 3)

Page 64, No. 2

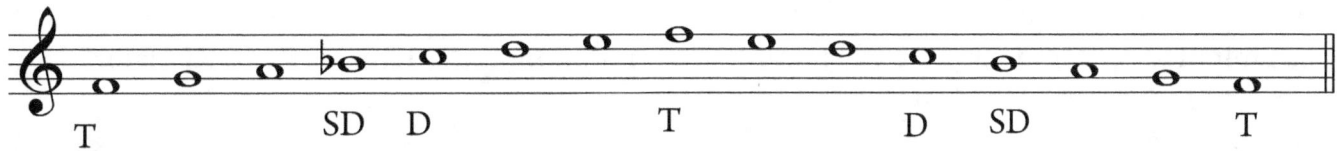

Page 65, No. 3

Page 65, No. 4

4/4   3/4   2/4

Page 66, No. 5

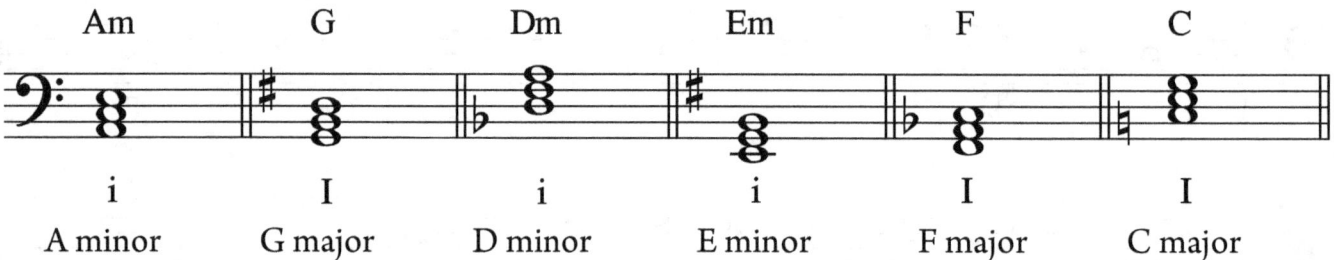

Page 66, No. 6

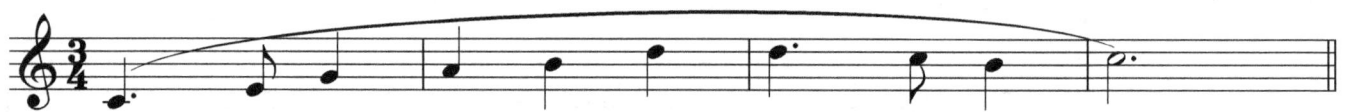

Page 66, No. 7

f, a, b, e, d, g, c

Page 67, No. 8

Study Op.125, No. 3

Anton Diabelli
(1781 - 1858)

a. Add the correct time signature directly on the music.

b. Name the key of this piece. **C major**

c. Name the composer of this piece. **Anton Diabelli**

d. Draw a phrase mark over each phrase.

e. On what scale degree does phrase one end? $\hat{2}$ Is this stable or unstable? **unstable**

f. On what degree does phrase two end? $\hat{1}$ Is this stable or unstable? **stable**

g. Define *Allegretto*. **Fairly fast, not as fast as allegro**

h. Name the triad at letter A. **C major**

i. Explain the sign at letter B. **Repeat sign, repeat from the beginning.**

Level 3

Page 2, No. 1

F# G♭	A# B♭	F E#
B♭ A#	B C♭	G♭ F#
C# D♭	G# A♭	D♭ C#
D# E♭	C B#	A♭ G#
E# F	B♭ A#	E♭ D#

Page 3, No. 2

Page 4, No. 1

Page 5, No. 1

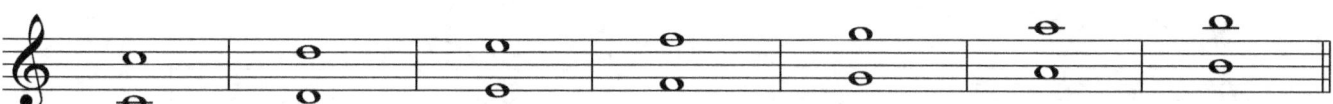

Page 5, No. 2

Page 6, No. 1

Page 6, No. 2

Page 6, No. 3

Page 9, No. 1

Page 9, No. 2

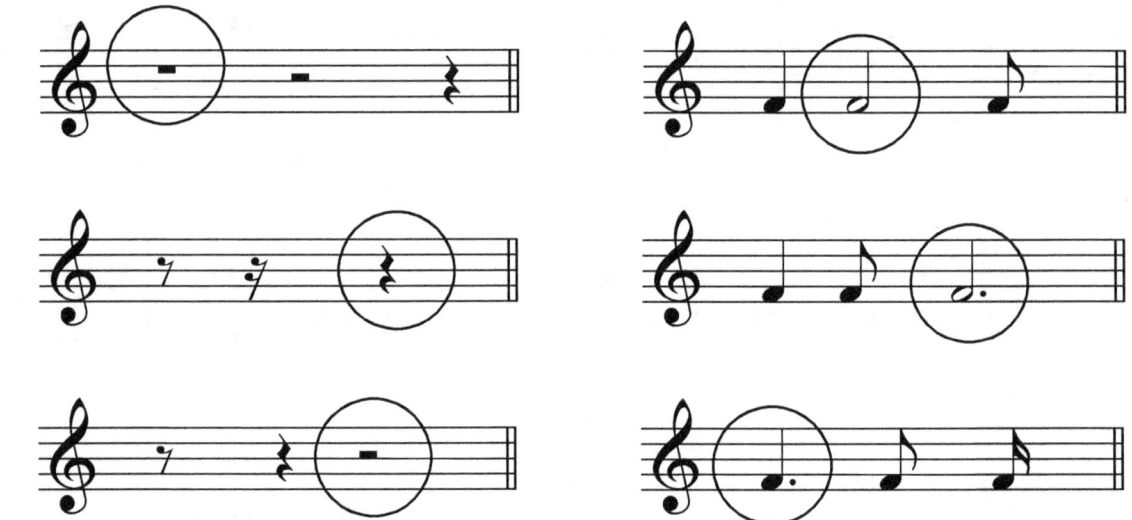

Page 10, No. 1

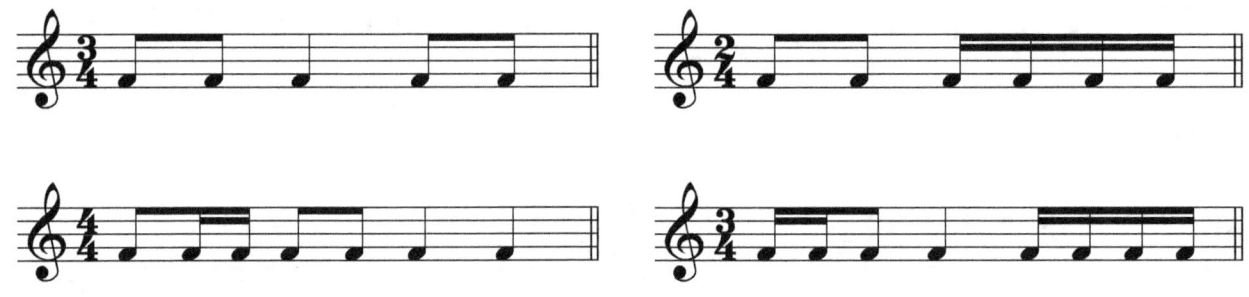

Page 11, No. 2

a) 2
b) 2
c) 2
d) 4
e) 2

Page 11, No. 3

Page 12, No. 4

3/4   3/4
2/4   2/4
4/4   4/4
3/4   4/4
2/4   3/4

Page 12, No. 5

Page 14, No. 1

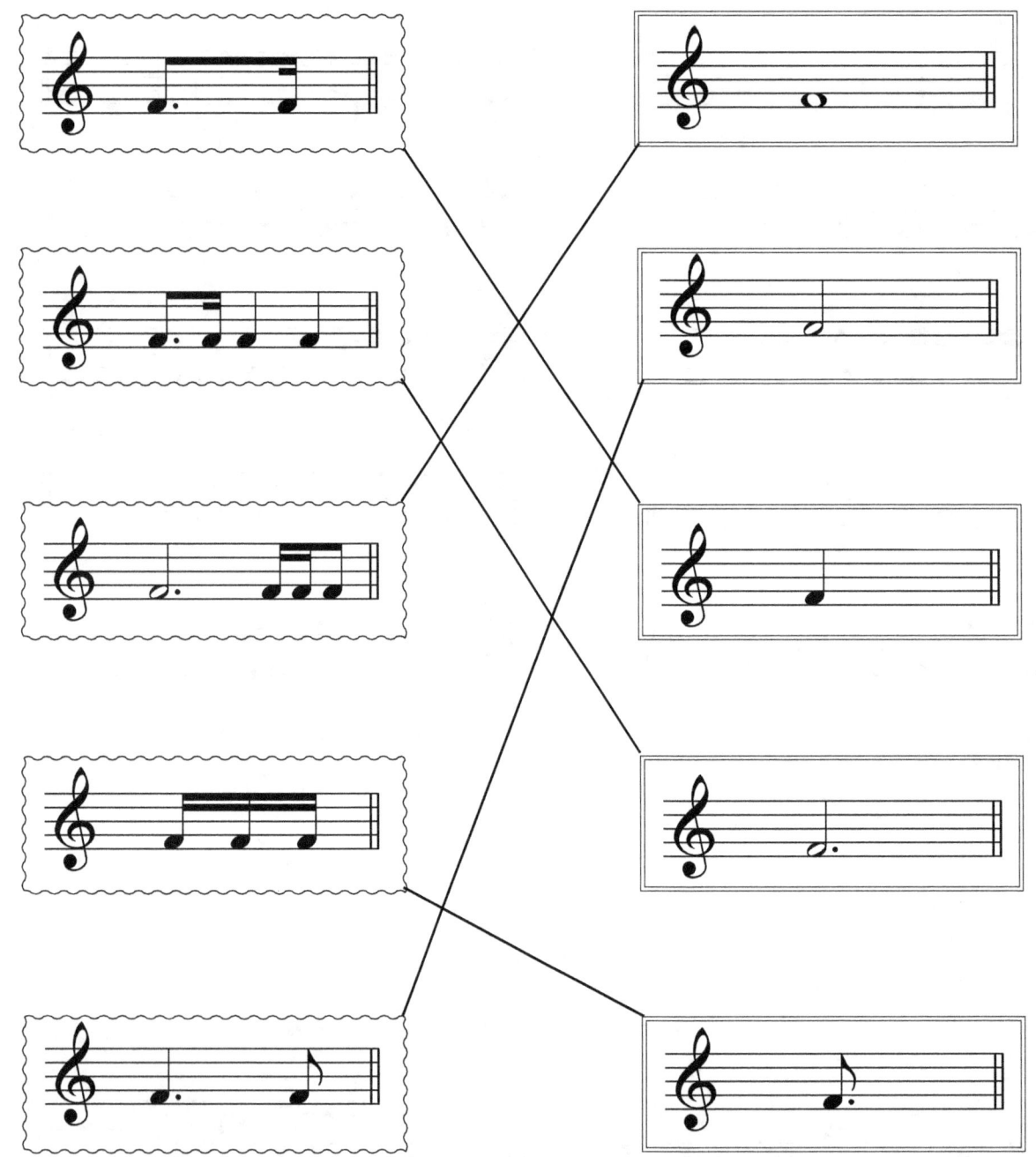

Page 15, No. 2

Bach
English Suite No. 2

Corelli
Concerto Grosso
Op. 6, No. 11

Mozart
Sonata in G

Liszt
Hungarian Rhapsody No. 14

Tchaikovsky
Swan Lake

Mozart
Trio in C

Bach
Brandenberg Concerto No. 2

© San Marco Publications 2022 — Level 3

Page 17, No. 1

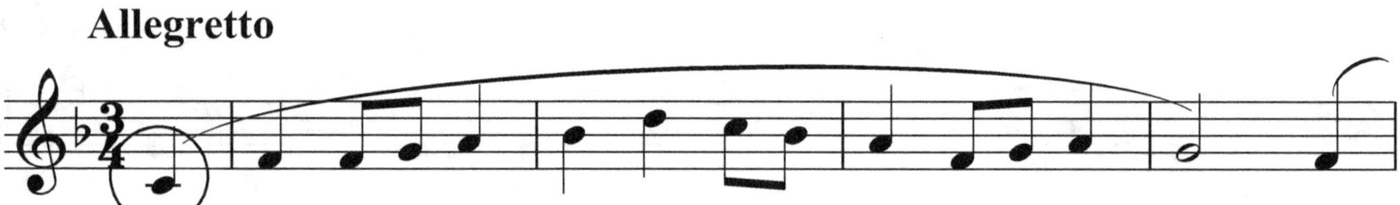

Allegretto

key: F major

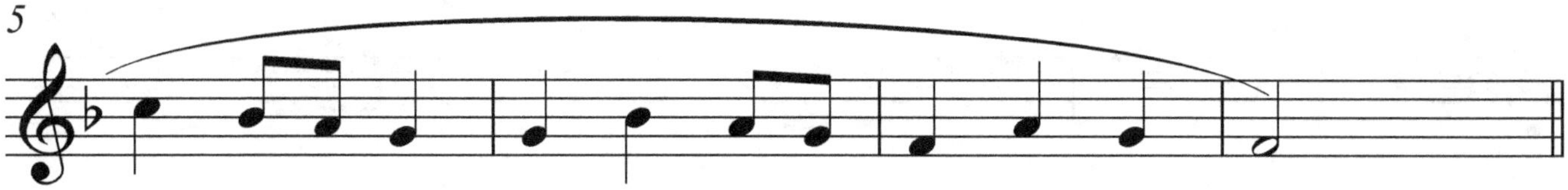

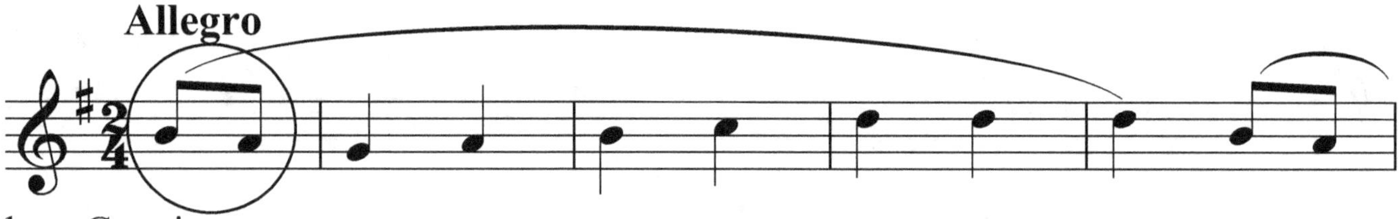

Allegro

key: G major

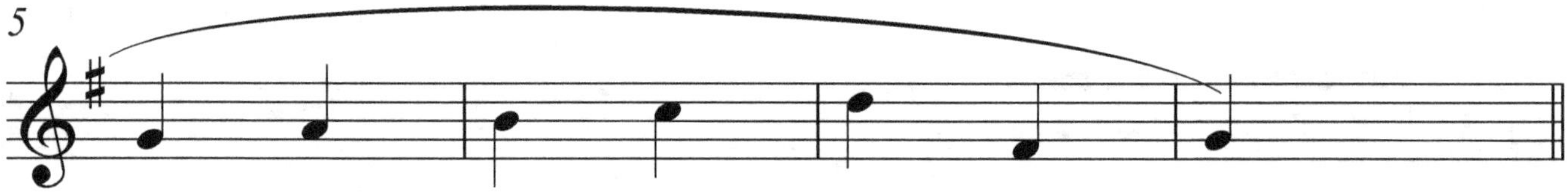

Page 20, No. 1

Page 20, No. 2

Page 21, No. 3

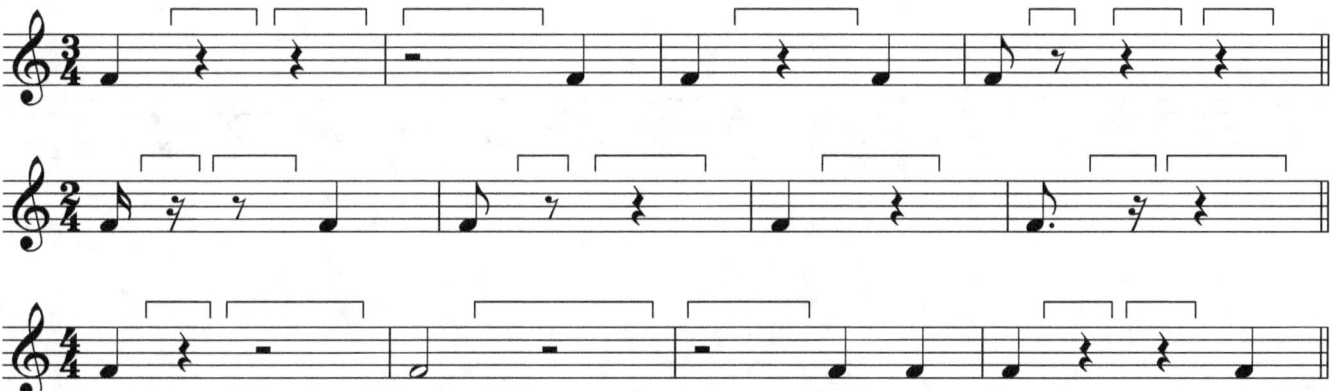

Page 21, No. 4

Page 23, No. 1

Page 24, No. 1

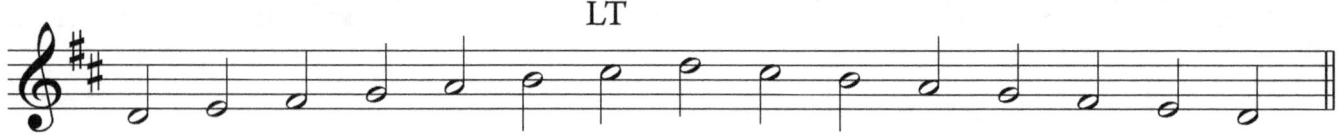

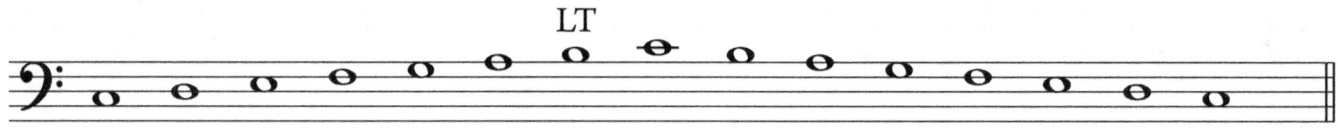

© San Marco Publications 2022   Level 3

Page 25, No. 2

B♭ major

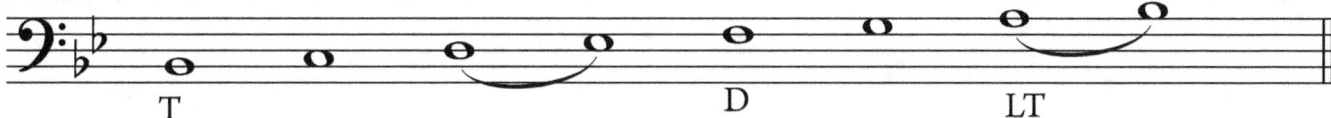

D major

F major

G major

C major

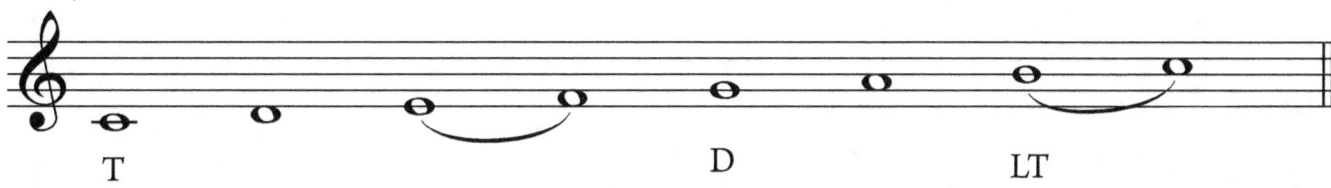

Page 26, No. 3

C major   B♭ major   D major   G major   F major

Page 26, No. 4

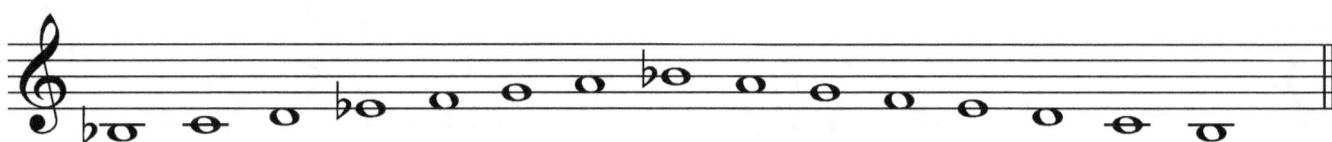

B♭ major

G major

F major

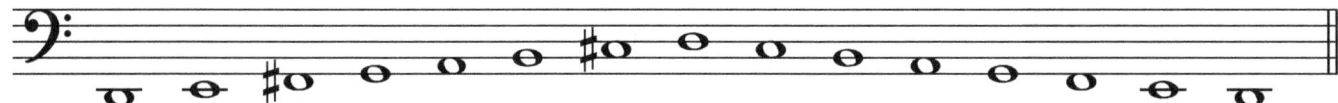

D major

Page 27, No. 5

E
D
E♭
D
B

Page 27, No. 6

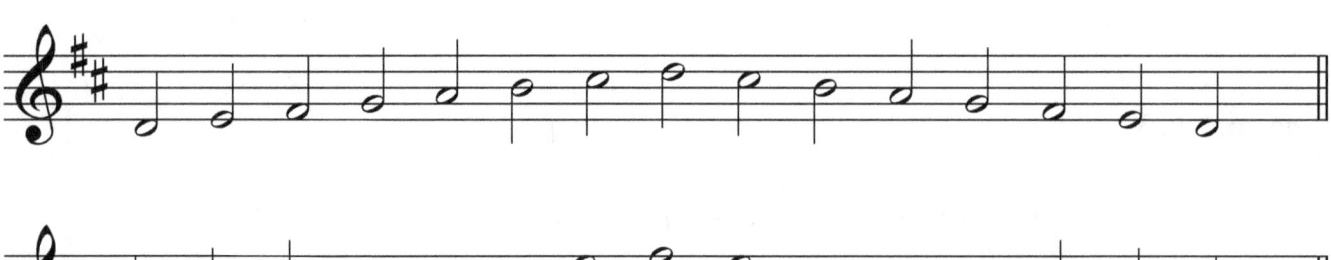

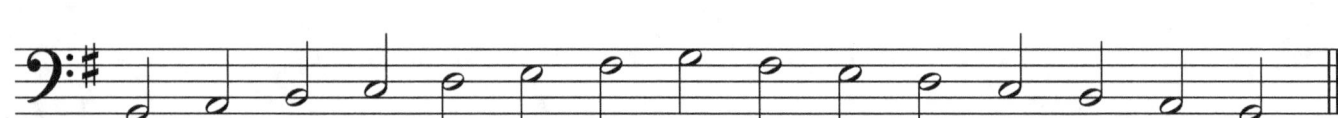

Page 30, No. 1 Review 1

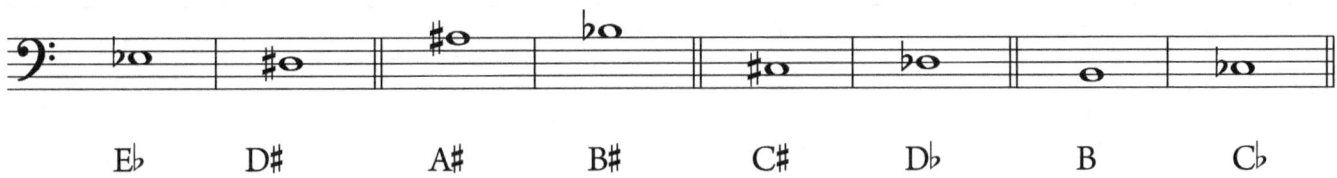

Page 30, No. 2

Page 30, No. 3

Page 31, No. 4

3/4
2/4
4/4
3/4

Page 31, No. 5

Page 32, No. 6

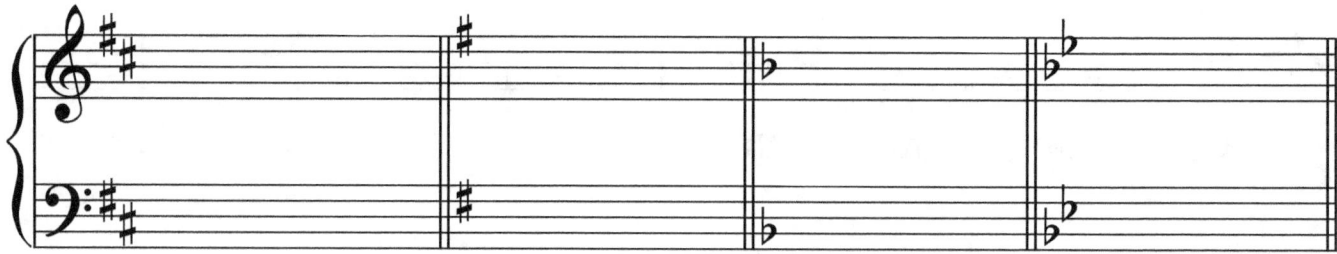

Page 32, No. 7

Page 32, No. 8

G major

Page 33, No. 9

a) Baroque
b) Johann Sebastian
c) Germany
d) Violin and Harpsichord
e) 20
f) Carl Phillip Emmanuel Bach, Johann Christian Bach
g) ☑ organist   ☑ cantor   ☐ pianist   ☑ composer   ☐ farmer   ☑ teacher
h) Felix Mendelssohn
i) 1750

Page 33, No. 10

d
c
e
a
b

Page 36, No. 1

D major **B minor**   B minor **D major**
E minor **G major**   A minor **C major**
C major **A minor**   G major **E minor**
F major **D minor**   D minor **F major**

Page 36, No. 2

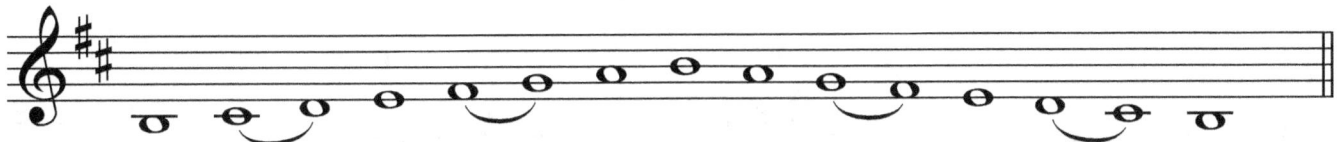

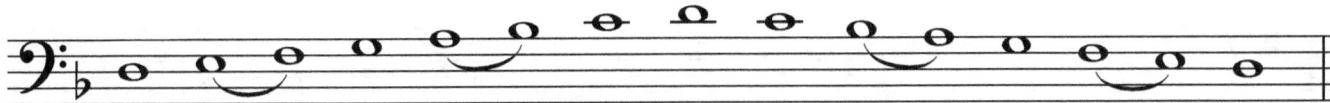

Page 38, No. 1

G minor

E minor

D minor

A minor

E minor

G minor

Page 39, No. 2

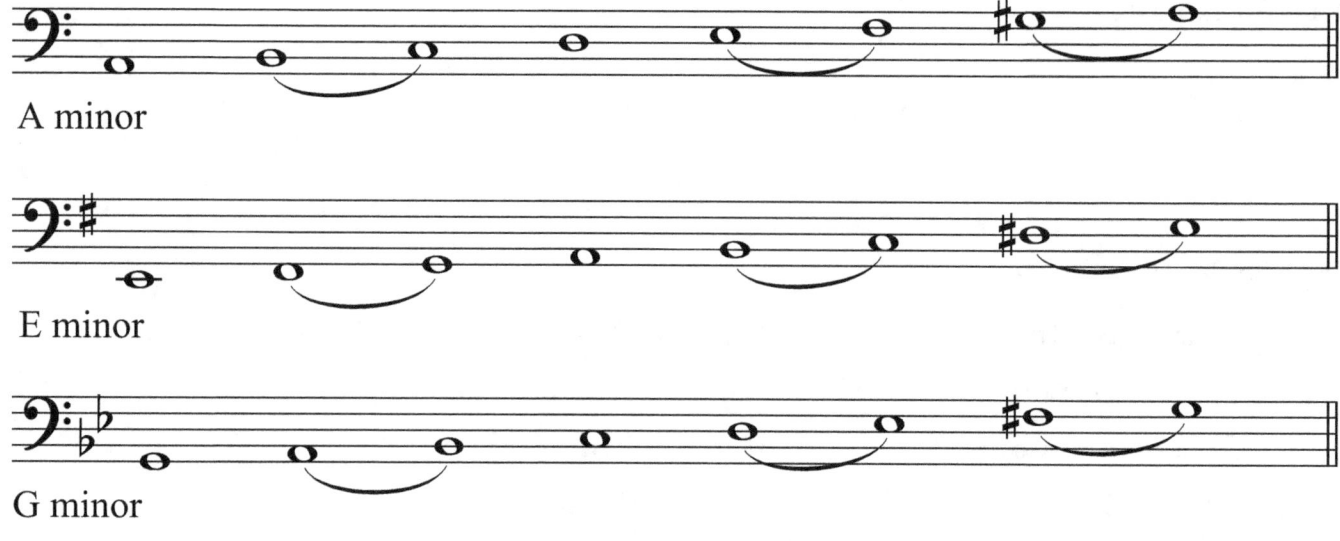

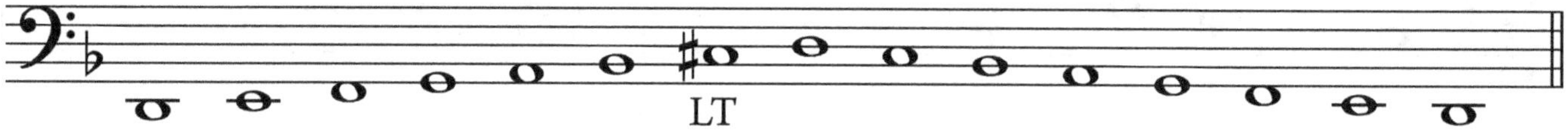

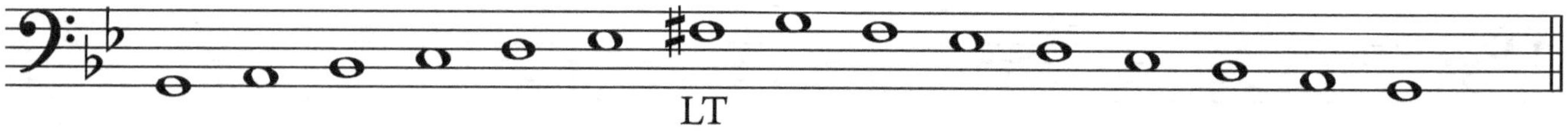

Page 41, No. 1

B minor

E minor

D minor

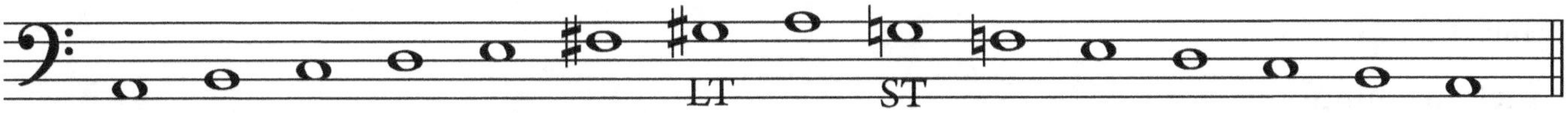

A minor

G minor

Page 42, No. 2

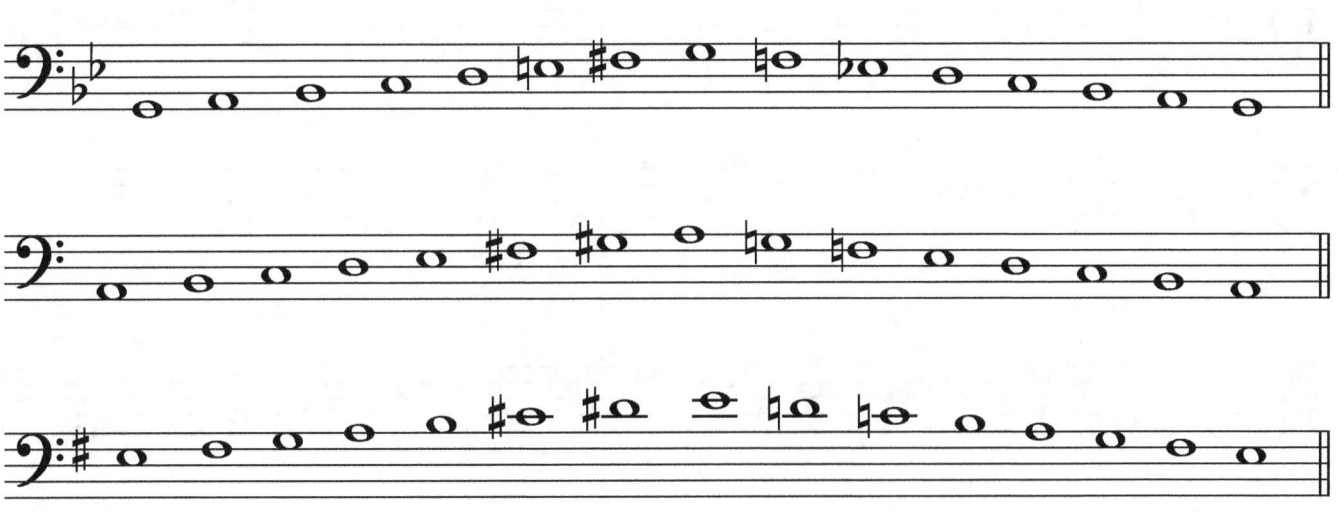

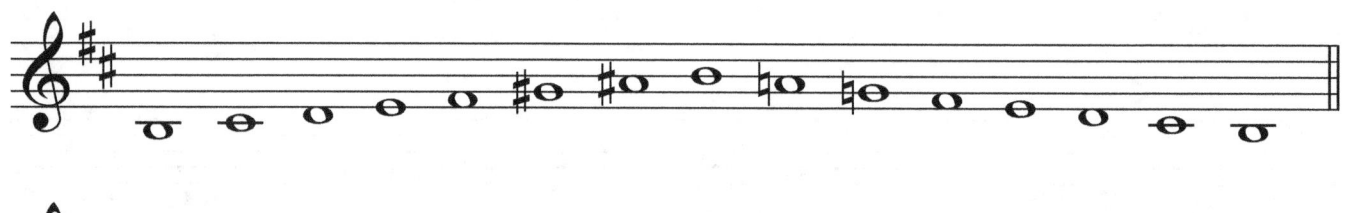

Page 43, No. 3

A harmonic minor

G natural minor

E melodic minor

D harmonic minor

B melodic minor

G melodic minor

Page 44, No. 4

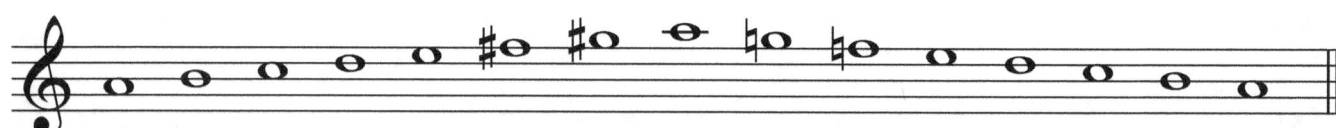

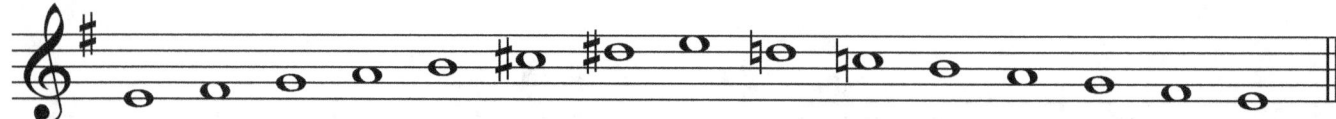

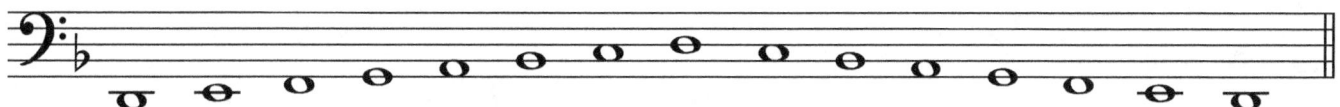

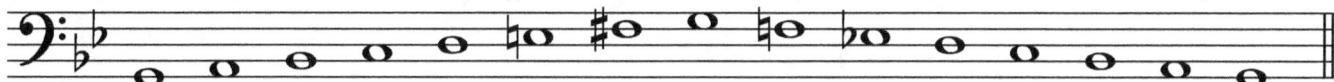

Page 45, No. 1

5 3 8 2 1 6

7 6 4 2 5 4

Page 46, No. 1

Page 47, No. 2

Page 47, No. 3

Page 47, No. 4

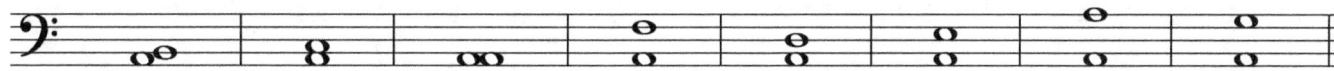

Page 47, No. 5

Page 50, No. 1

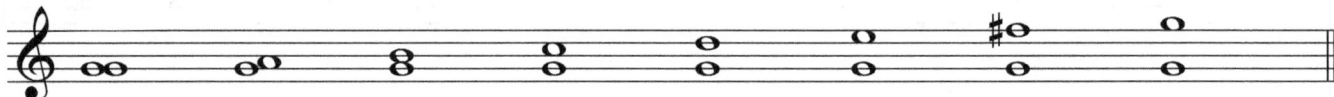

Page 50, No. 2

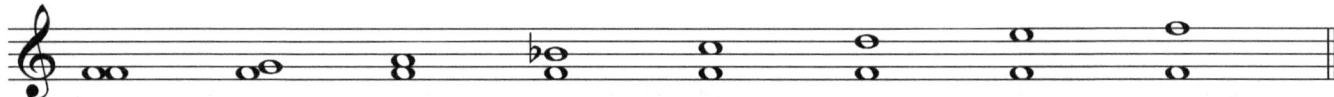

Page 50, No. 3

maj 6   per 4   maj 7   per 8   maj 2   per 4

maj 7   maj 3   per 4   per 5   per 8   per 1

Page 51, No. 4

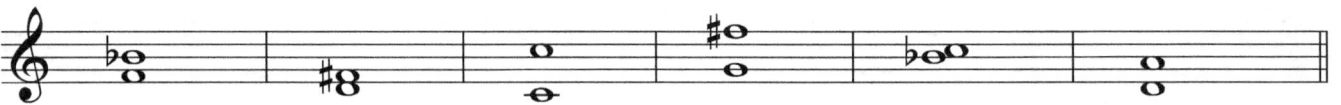

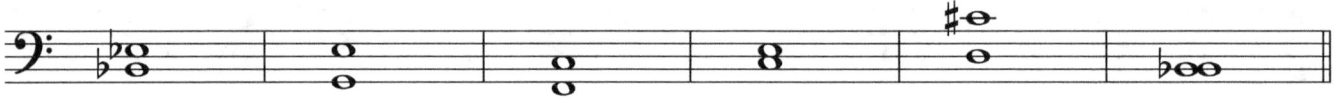

Page 51, No. 5

© San Marco Publications 2022   69   Level 3

Page 52, No. 1

Page 52, No. 2

min 3   min 3   maj 3   min 3   maj 3
maj 3   min 3   maj 3   maj 3   min 3

Page 53, No. 3

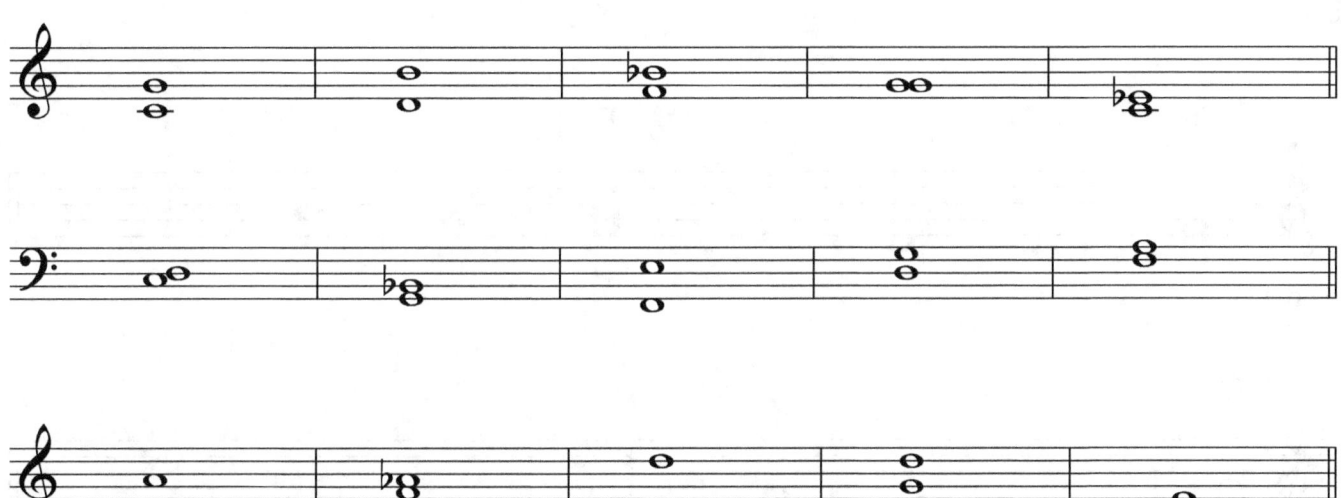

Page 53, No. 4

min 3   per 5   maj 2   maj 7   per 5
maj 3   min 3   per 8   maj 6   maj 7
min 3   per 4   maj 7   min 3   maj 6

Page 55, No. 1

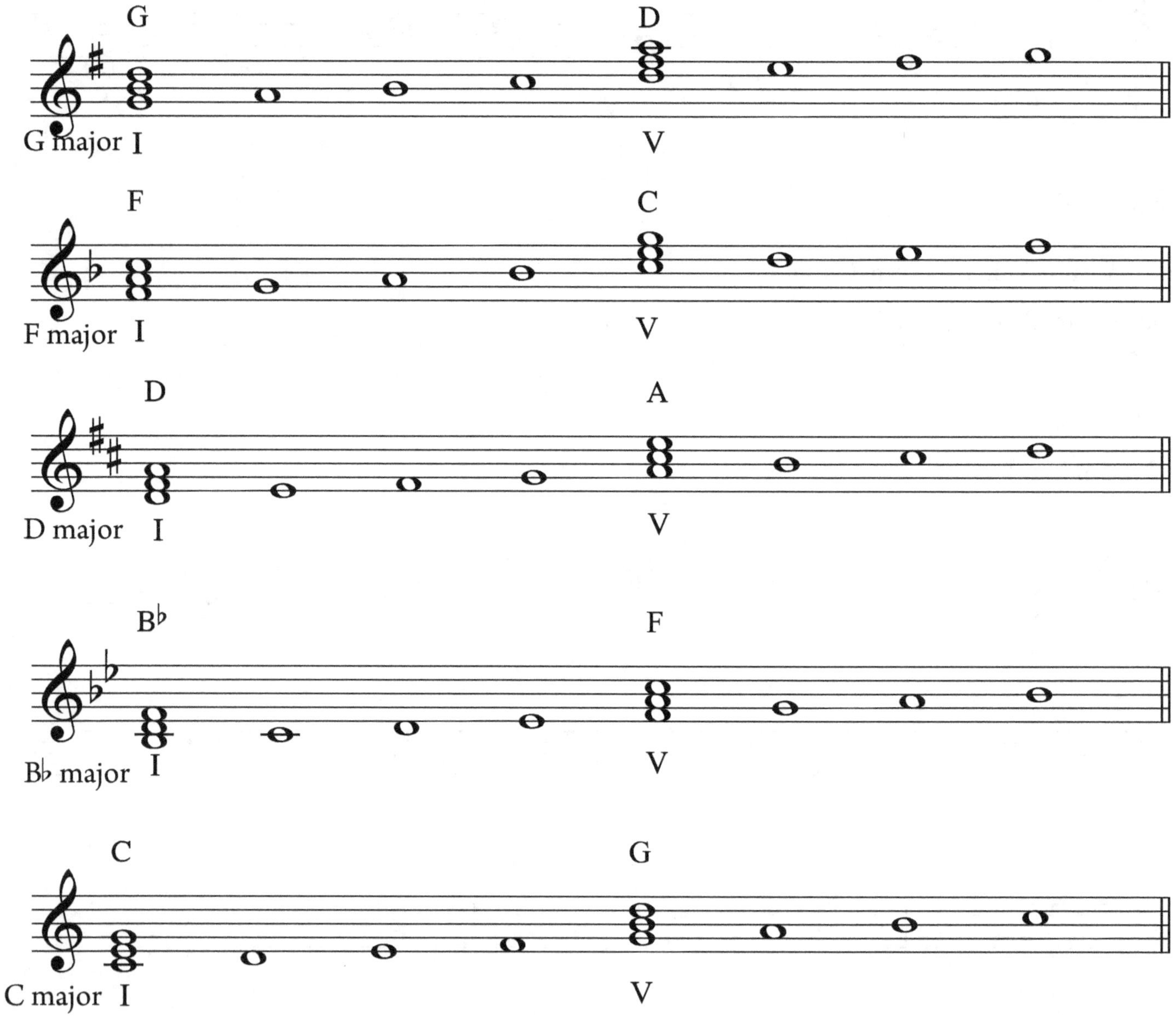

Page 56, No. 2

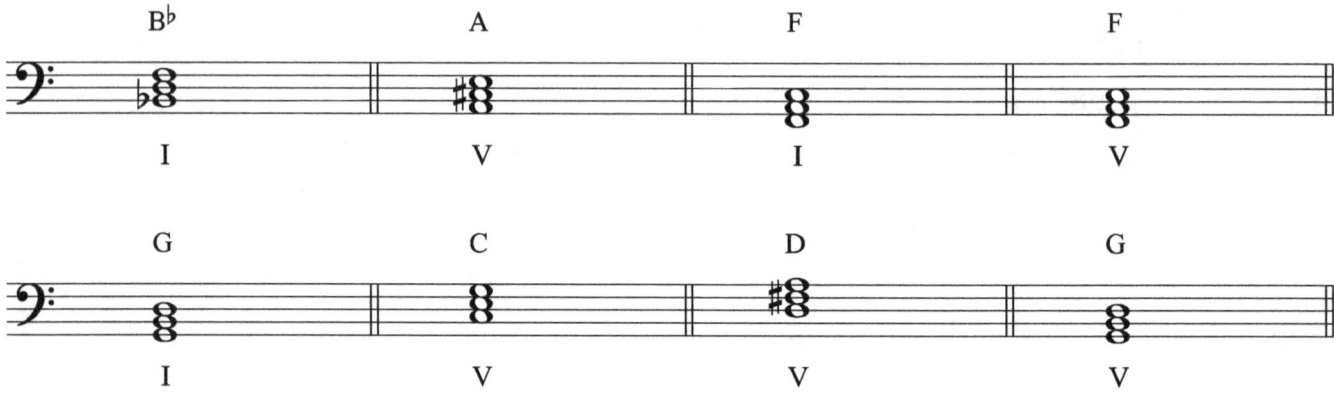

Page 57, No. 1

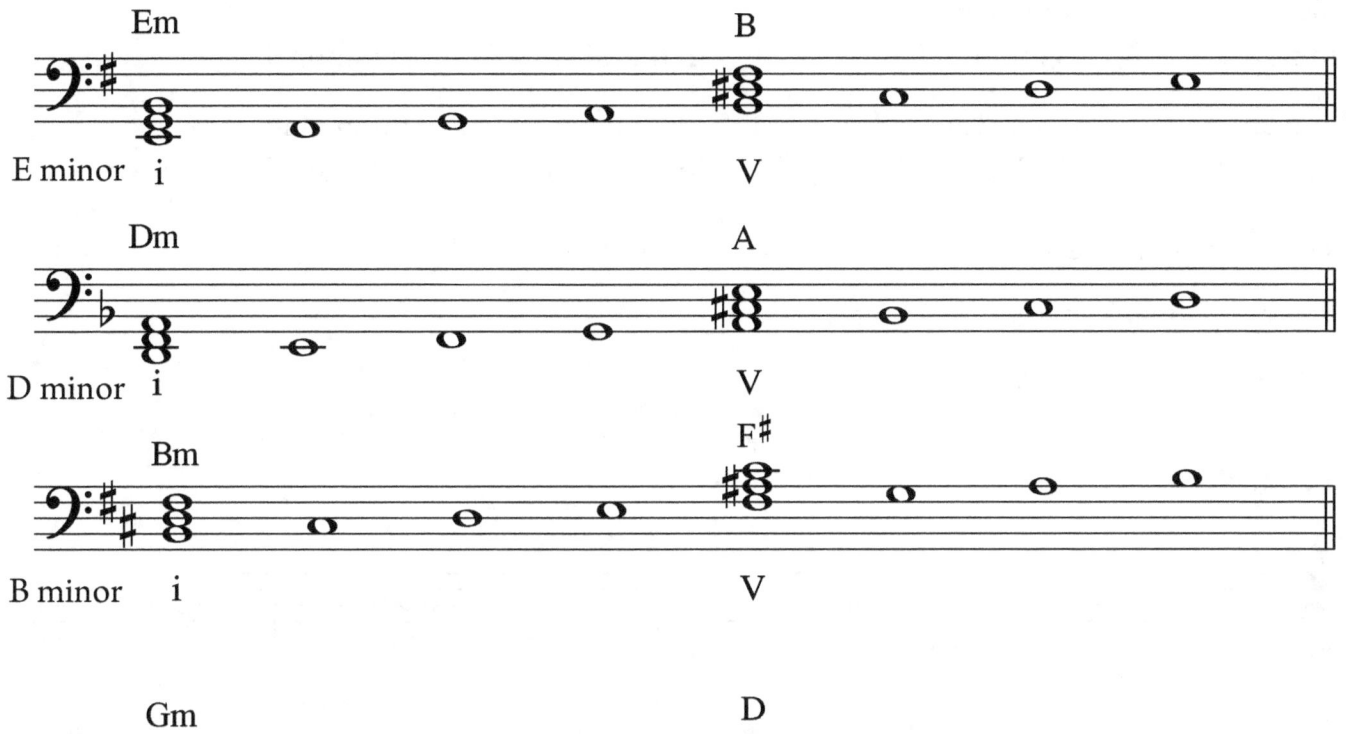

Page 58, No. 2

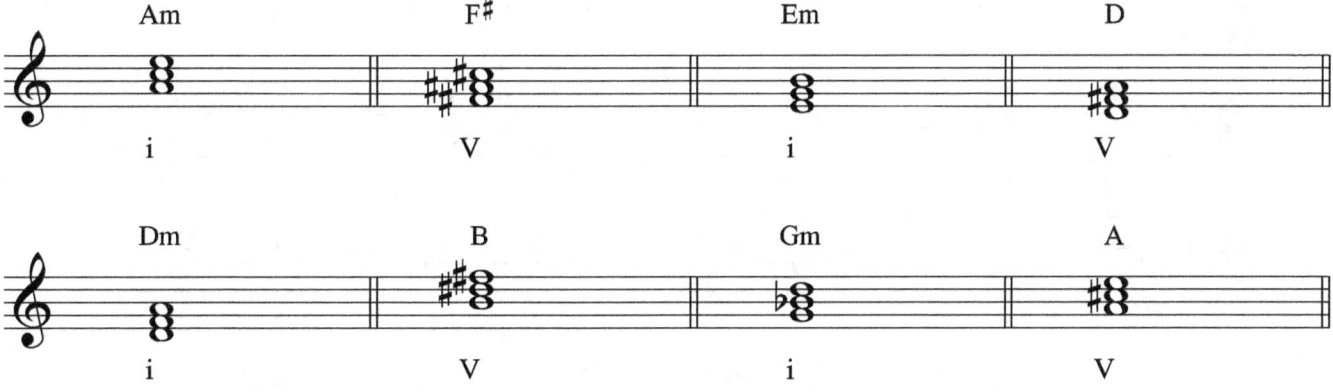

Page 58, No. 3

tonic	dominant	tonic	tonic
A minor i	D minor V	B minor i	E minor i
dominant	dominant	dominant	dominant
G minor V	E minor V	A minor V	B minor V

Page 61, No. 1   Review 2

per 4   maj 7   maj 3   per 5   maj 2   maj 6

per 8   per 1   maj 3   per 5   per 4   maj 6

Page 61, No. 2

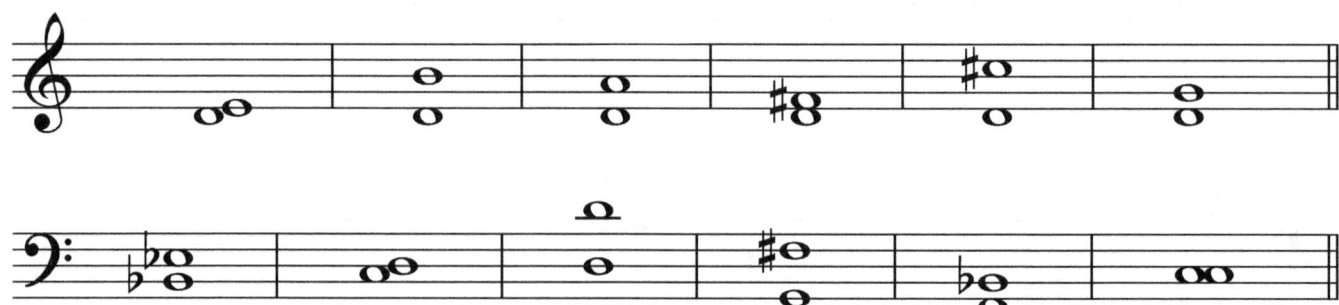

Page 62, No. 3

Page 63, No. 4

Page 63, No. 5

marcato	marked, stressed
cantabile	in a singing style
maestoso	majestically
grazioso	gracefully
dolce	sweetly
ottava	the interval of an octave
dal segno	from the sign

Page 64, No. 6

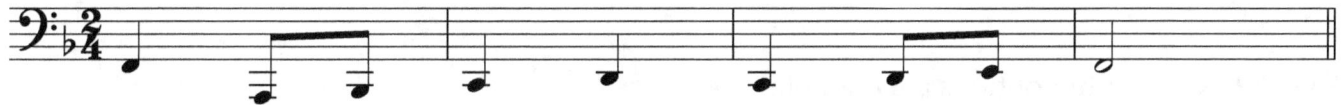

Page 64, No. 7

a) Johann Sebastian Bach
b) Bach's second wife
c) Carl Phillip Emmanuel Bach, Johann Christian Bach
d) Dances, Arias, Chorales
e) Harpsichord
f) Keyboard

Page 68, No. 1 (other options are possible)

Page 68, No. 2 (other options are possible)

Page 68, No. 3 (other options are possible)

Page 69, No. 4 (other options are possible)

Page 69, No. 5 (other options are possible)

© San Marco Publications 2022   Level 3

Page 71-72, No. 1

Page 73

Allegro

Alexander Reinagle
(1756 - 1809)

a. Add the correct time signature directly on the music.

b. Name the key of this piece. **C major**

c. Name the composer of this piece. **Alexander Reinagle**

d. Draw a phrase mark over each phrase.

e. Label the phrases according to the form (a, a¹, b)

f. These two phrases form a: ☑ contrasting period ☐ parallel period

g. Does the second phrase end on a stable or unstable degree? **stable**

h. Define *Allegro*. **fast**

i. How are measure 1 and 2 similar to 5 and 6? **The rhythm is the same.**

i. Locate and circle a half step in this piece.

Page 74

Carefree

Daniel Gottlob Turk
((1756 - 1813))

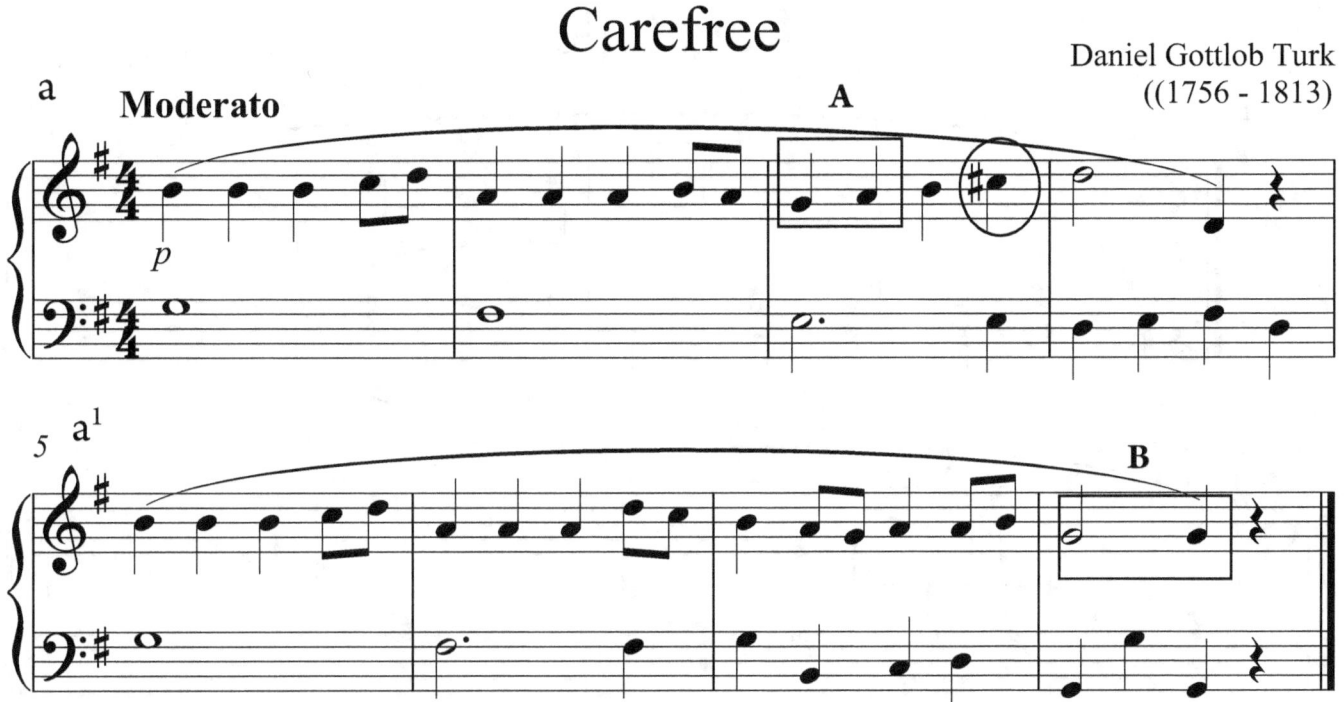

a. Add the correct time signature directly on the music.

b. Name the key of this piece. **G major**

c. Name the composer of this piece. **Daniel Gottlob Turk**

d. Draw a phrase mark over each phrase.

e. Label the phrases according to the form (a, a¹, b)

f. These two phrases form a: ☐ contrasting period ☑ parallel period

g. Does the second phrase end on a stable or unstable degree? **stable**

h. Define *Moderato*. **at a moderate speed**

i. Find and circle one accidental in this piece.

j. Name the interval at letter A. **maj 2**

k. Name the interval at letter B. **per 1**

© San Marco Publications 2022   Level 3

Page 75

Bagatelle

Anton Diabelli

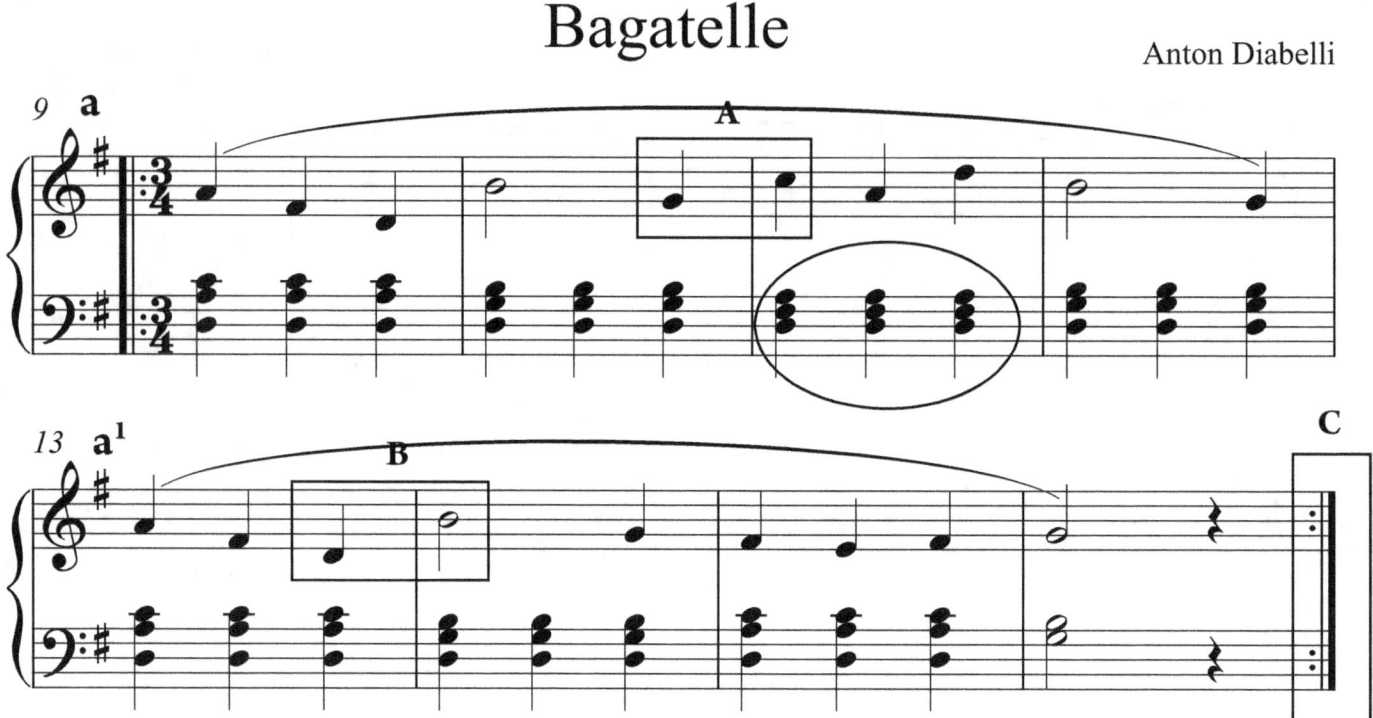

a. Add the correct time signature directly on the music.

b. Name the key of this piece. **G major**

c. Name the composer of this piece. **Anton Diabelli**

d. Draw a phrase mark over each phrase.

e. Label the phrases according to the form (a, a¹, b)

f. Does the second phrase end on a stable or unstable degree? **stable**

g. Find and circle one dominant triad in this piece.

h. Name the interval at letter A. **per 4**

i. Name the interval at letter B. **maj 6**

j. Explain the sign at letter C. **Repeat sign. Repeat the music between the repeat signs.**

k. On what measure does this piece begin? **9**

Page 79, No. 1   Review 3

per 5   maj 2   maj 7   maj 6   min 3   per 1

maj 3   per 4   per 8   maj 7   maj 6   maj 2

Page 79, No. 2

Page 80, No. 3

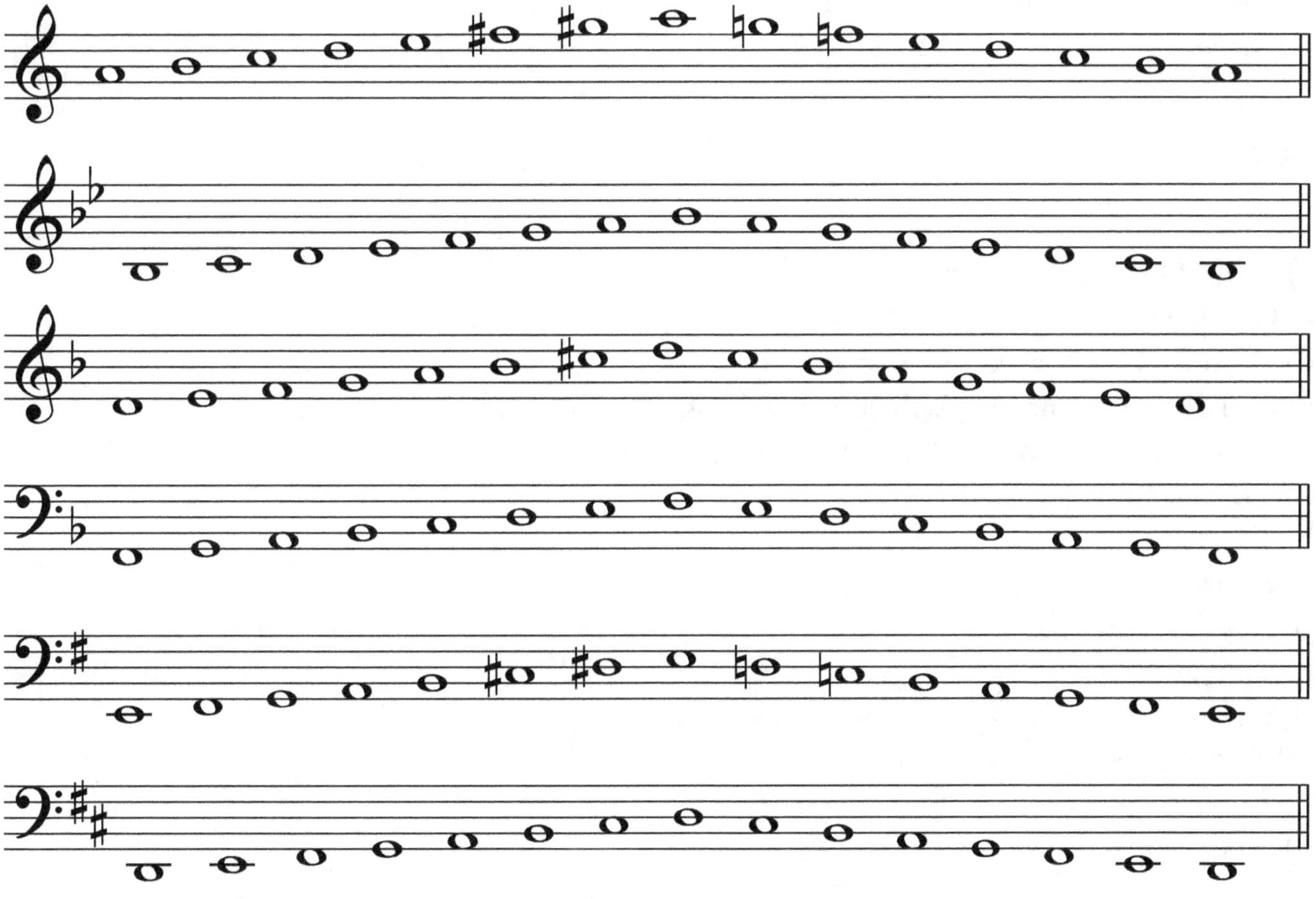

Page 81, No. 4

Page 81, No. 5

Page 81, No. 6

marcato	marked or stressed
grazioso	graceful
dolce	sweet
maestoso	majestic
cantabile	in a singing style
ottava	the interval of an octave
dal segno	from the sign

Page 82, No. 7

a) Baroque
b) 1600 -1750
c) Germany
d) A book of Baroque keyboard pieces
e) Carl Phillip Emmanuel Bach, Johann Christian Bach
f) Dances, Arias, Chorales, Minuet, Gavotte, Gigue
g) Harpsichord
h) Keyboard
i) France
j) 3/4
k) France
l) Yes
m) Allegro, Presto
n) three
o) At the end

Level 4

Page 4, No. 1

Page 4, No. 2

Page 4, No. 3

Page 6, No. 1

Mikhail Glinka
Souvenir of a Night in Madrid

Page 6, No. 2

Wolfgang Amadeus Mozart
Piano Concerto K270

Page 8, No. 1

Page 8, No. 2

3/4	3/4
2/4	2/4
4/4	4/4
3/4	4/4
2/4	3/4

Page 10, No. 1

Page 10, No. 2

3/4
2/4
4/4
3/4

Page 12, No. 1

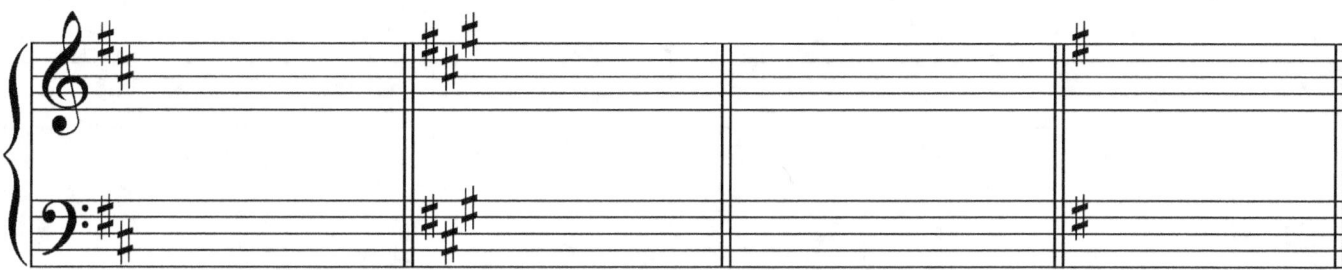

Page 12, No. 2

Page 14, No. 1

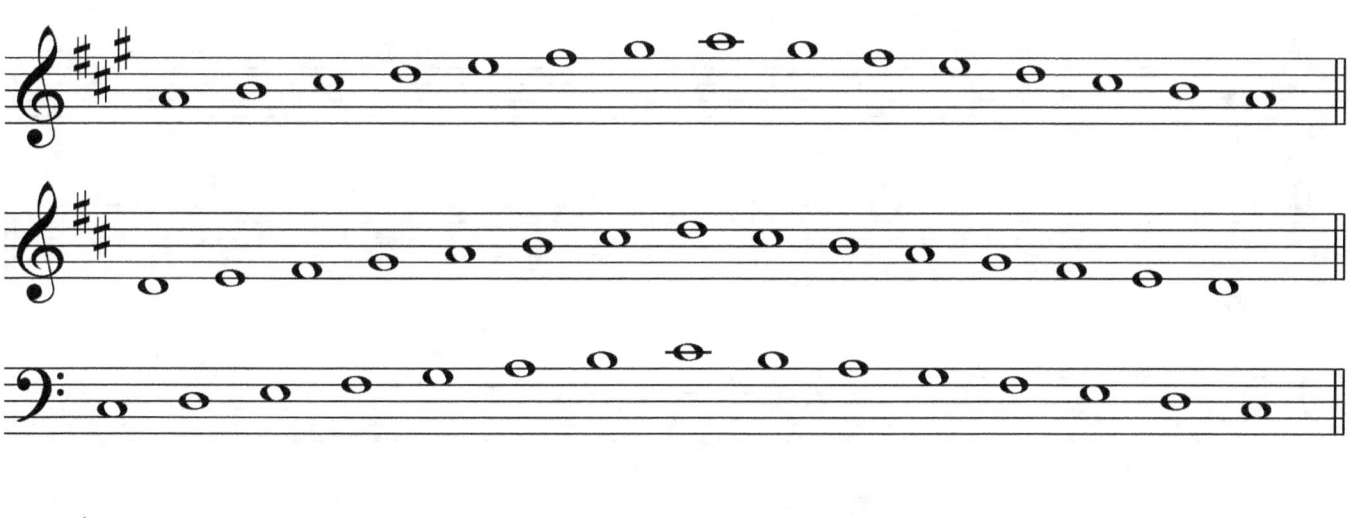

Page 15, No. 1

Page 16, No. 2 (other options for this question are possible)

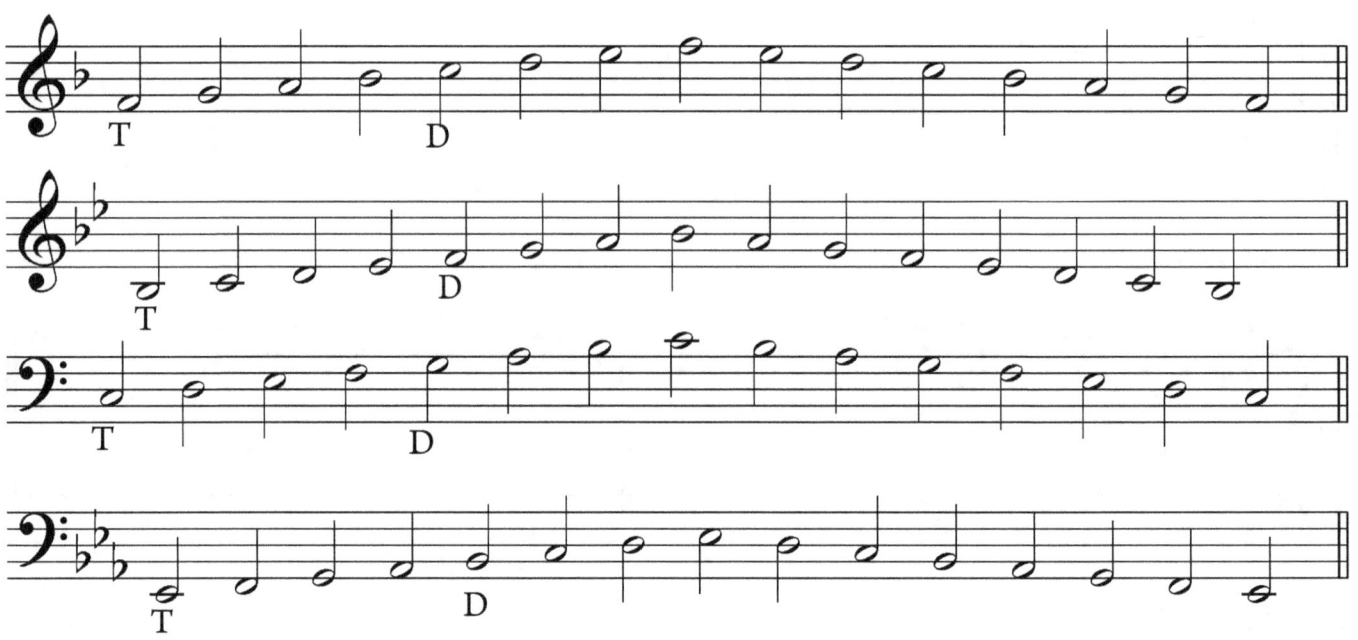

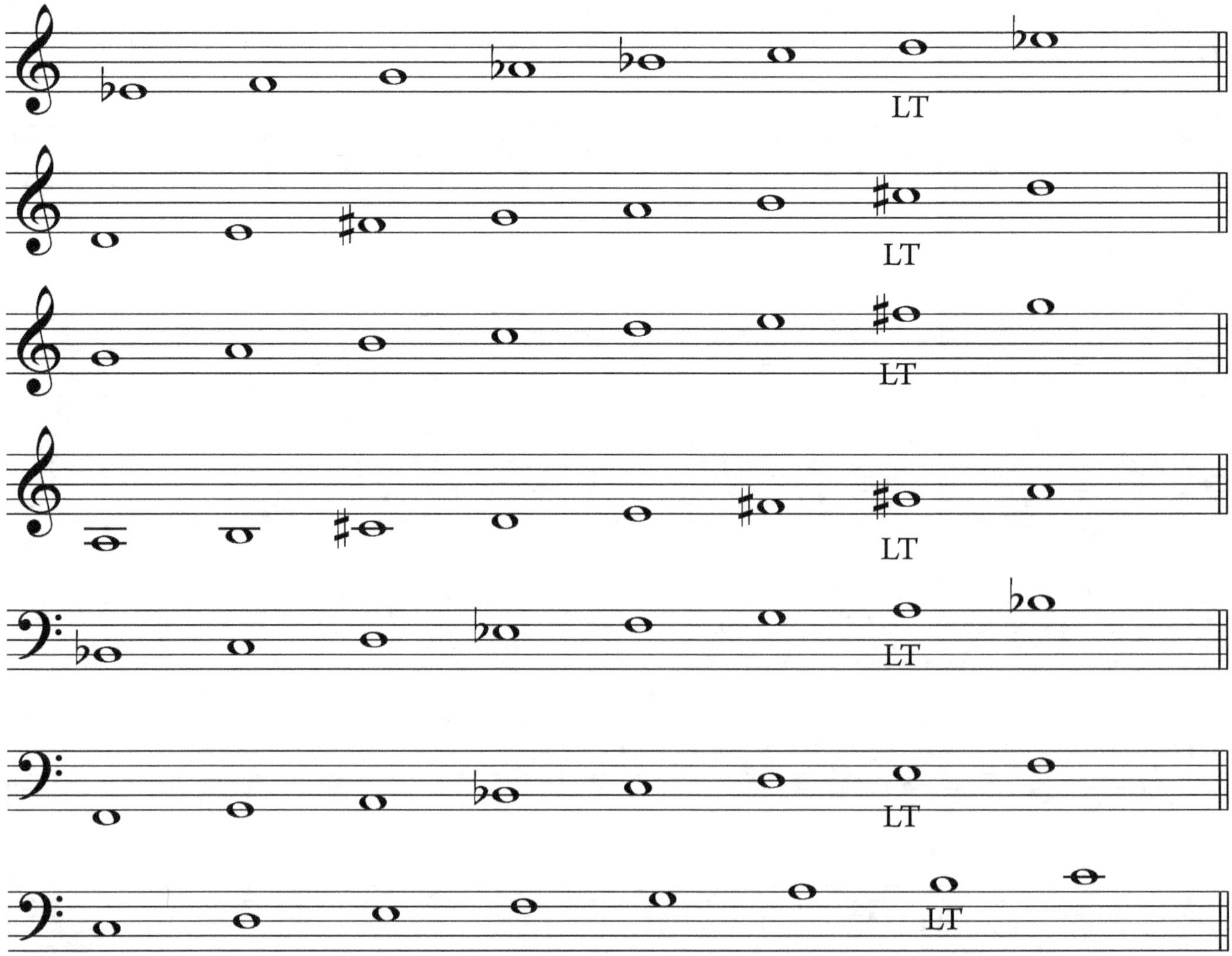

© San Marco Publications 2022   85   Level 4

Page 17, No. 3

Page 21, No. 1 Review 1

Page 21, No. 2

Claude Debussy
Prelude "Voiles"

Page 21, No. 3

Page 22, No. 4

Page 22, No. 5

4/4	4/4
2/4	3/4
3/4	2/4
2/4	4/4

Level 4

Page 23, No. 6

Page 23, No. 7

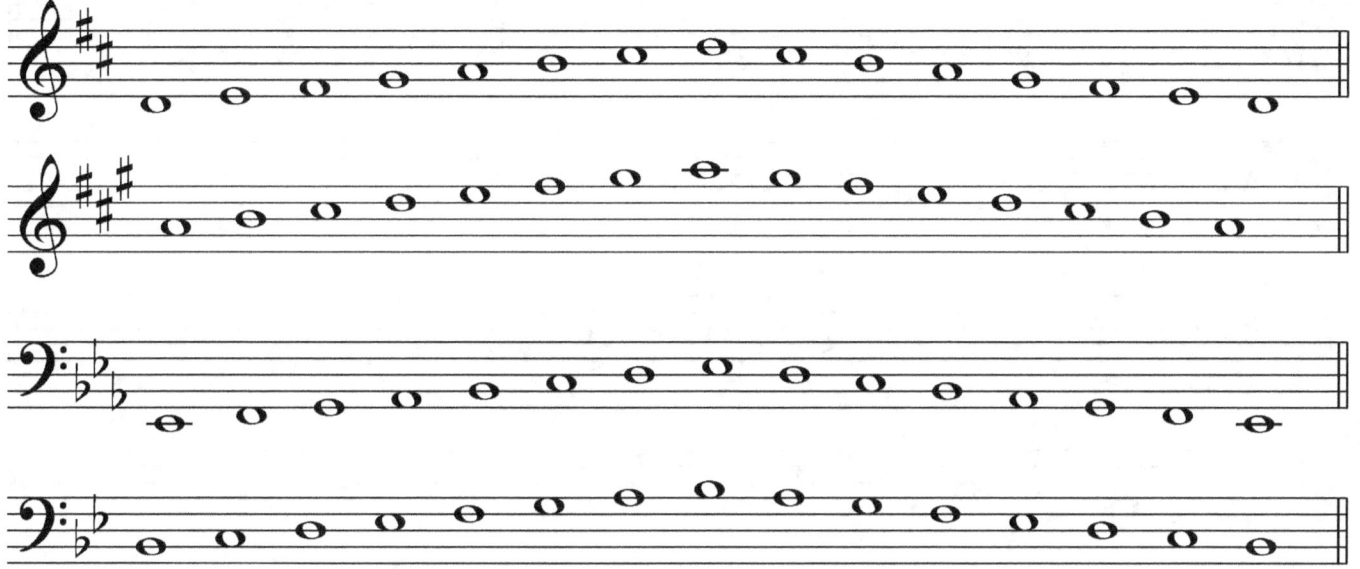

Page 24, No. 8

1. **Strings** (violin, viola, cello, double bass, harp)

2. **Woodwinds** (flute, clarinet, oboe, bassoon, piccolo, saxophone, double bassoon)

3. **Brass** (horn, trumpet, trombone, tuba)

4. **Percussion** (Bass drum, Chimes, Gong, Triangle, Cymbals, Snare drum, Tambourine, Drum, Timpani, Xylophone, Marimba)

Page 24, No. 9

cantabile	in a singing style
dolce	sweetly
grazioso	gracefully
maestoso	majestically
marcato	marked or stressed

Page 27, No. 1

D minor	F major	B♭ major	G minor
E minor	G major	C major	A minor
B minor	D major	D major	B minor
C minor	E♭ major	E♭ major	C minor
F# minor	A major	A major	F# minor

Page 29, No. 1

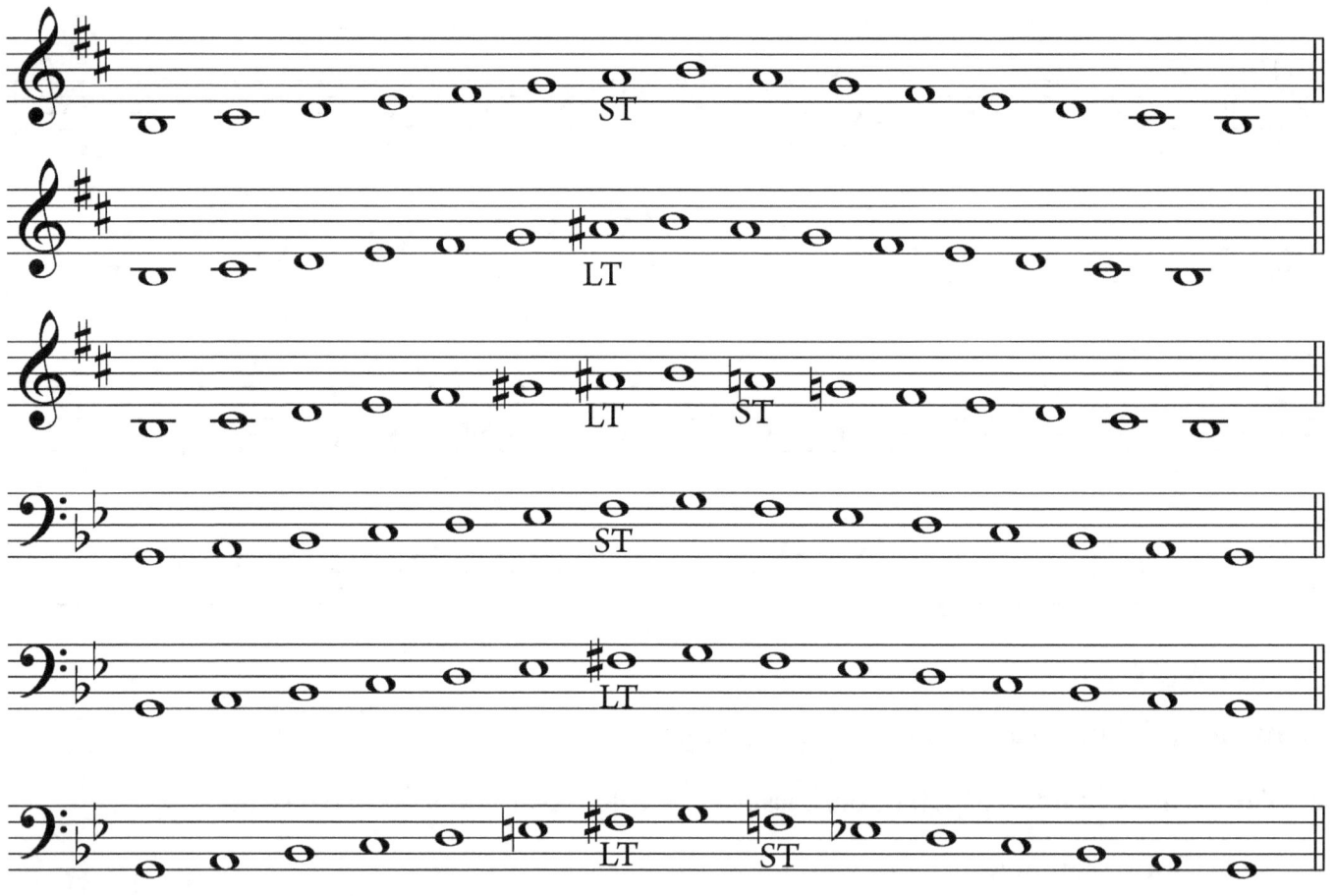

Page 30, No. 2

E natural minor
C harmonic minor
F# melodic minor
D harmonic minor
A harmonic minor
B harmonic minor
G melodic minor

Page 31, No. 3

Page 33, No. 1

per 5, maj 3, maj 6, maj 2, per 8, maj 7, maj 6

per 1, per 4, maj 6, maj 3, per 5, per 8, maj 2

Page 34, No. 1

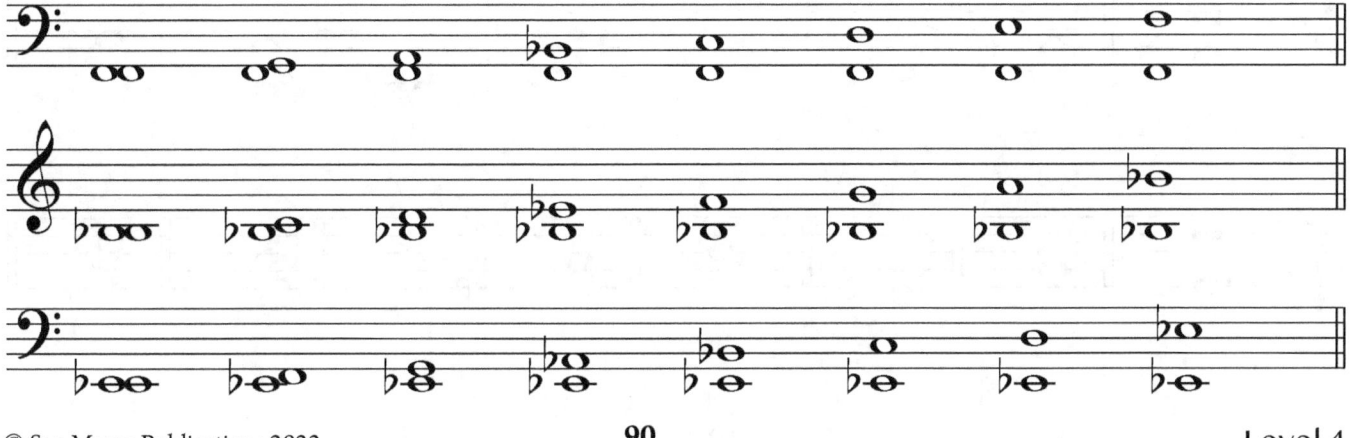

Page 35, No. 1

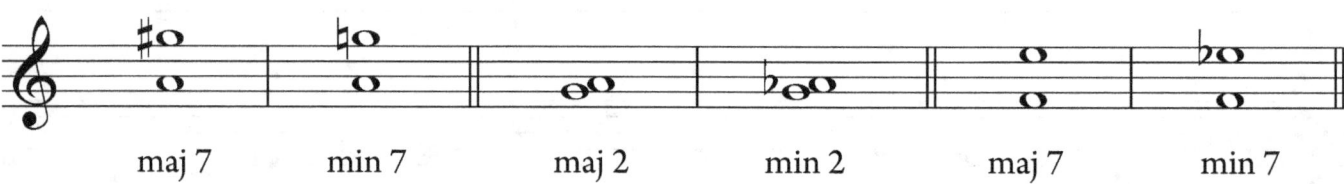

Page 36, No. 2

maj 6, per 4, maj 3, min 7, min 7, min 6, per 5

maj 2, per 4, min 6, min 7, maj 3, maj 3, per 4

Page 37, No. 3

Page 37, No. 4

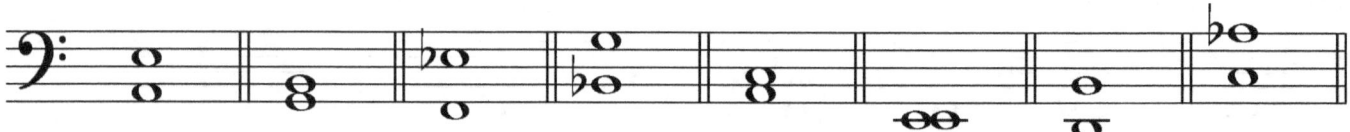

Page 38, No. 5

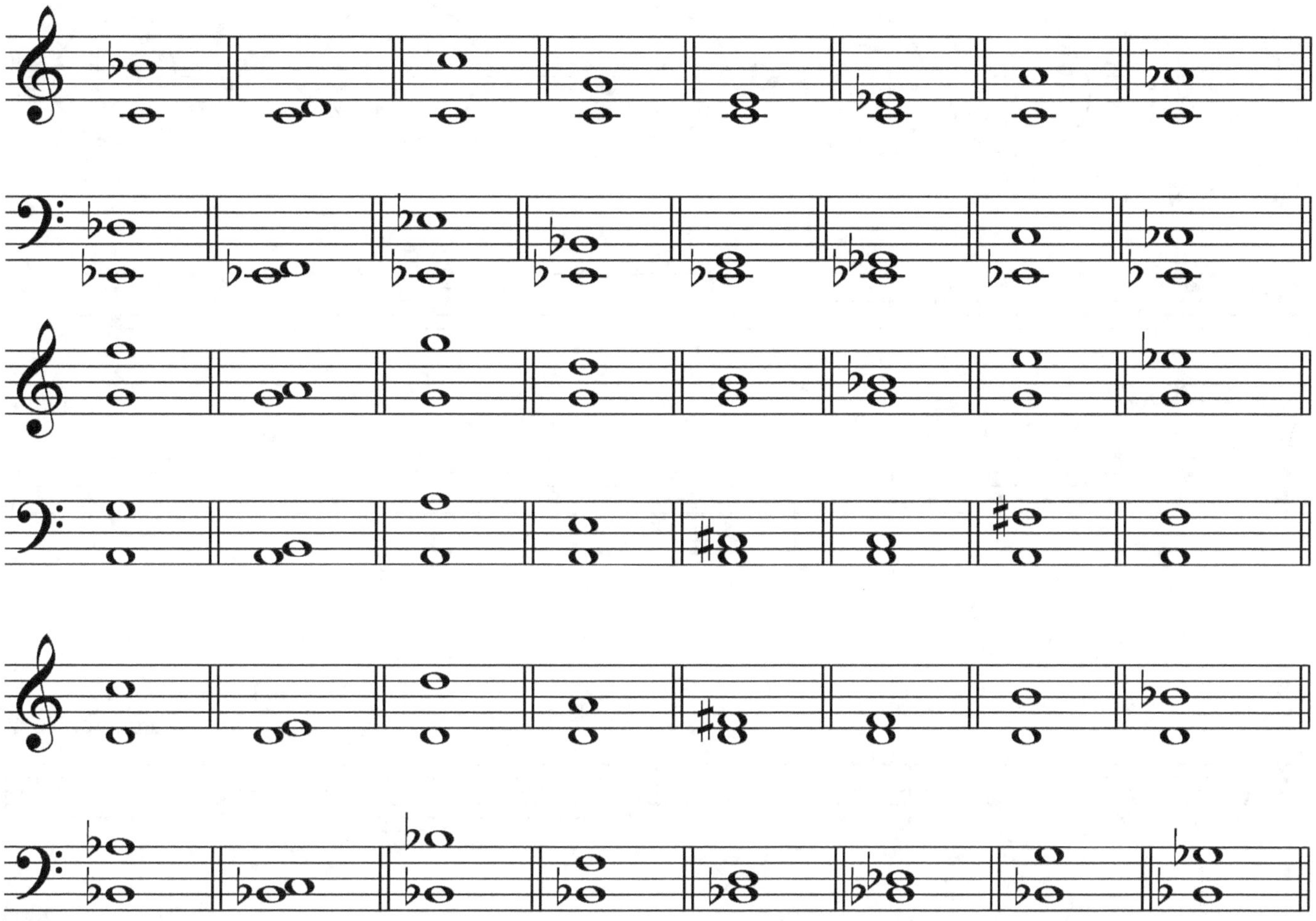

Page 39, No. 6

min 7, maj 6

maj 2, maj 2, per 1

maj 3, maj 2, min 3, min 3

per 5, maj 2, min 2, maj 2, min 2, maj 2

Page 40, No. 1

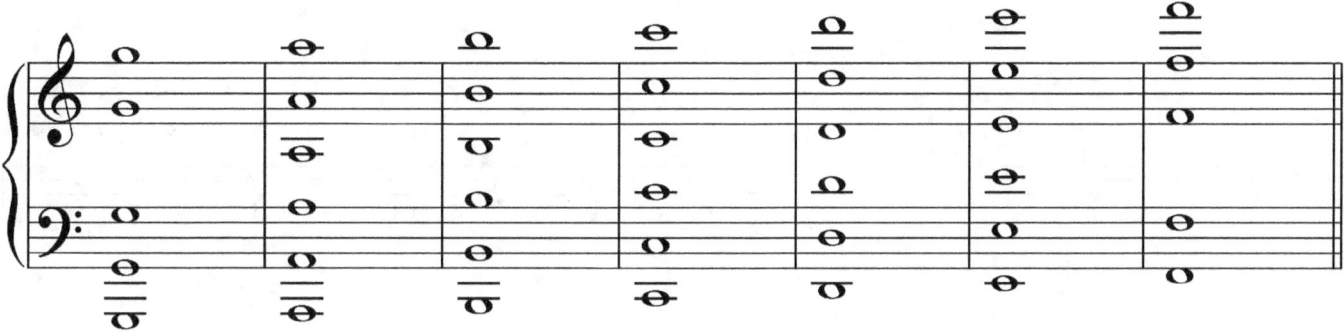

Page 40, No. 2

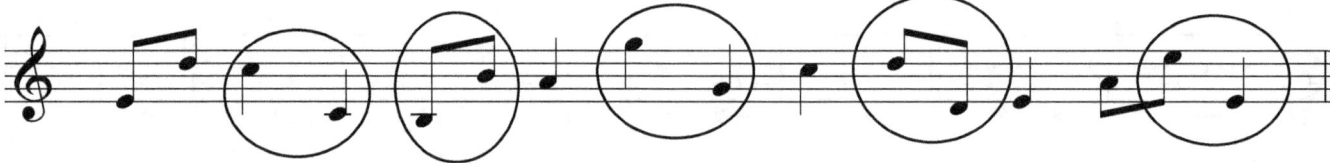

Page 42, No. 1

Page 43, No. 2

Page 43, No. 3

Ludwig van Beethoven
Leonore, No. 2

Enrique Granados
Spanish Dance, No. 6

Page 44, No. 4

Johannes Brahms
Seranade in D, V

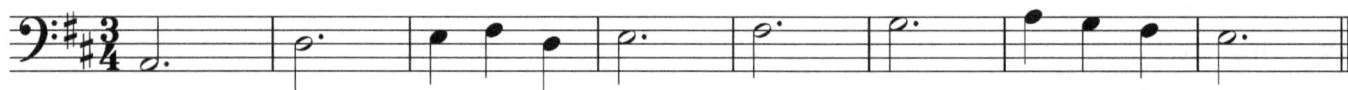

Frederic Chopin
Nocturne Op. 72, No. 1

Page 47, No. 1

4/8 or 2/4
2/8
3/8
4/8 or 2/4
2/8
3/8

Page 48, No. 2

Page 49, No. 3

Page 50, No. 4

Page 53, No. 1

Page 53, No. 2

Page 54, No. 3

Page 58, No. 1 Review 2

Page 59, No. 2

Page 59, No. 3

Page 59, No. 4

per 4, maj 7, min 3, per 8, maj 7, maj 2, min 6, per 8

Page 59, No. 5

Page 60, No. 6

Page 60, No. 7

William Byrd
Pavan

Page 60, No. 8

Felix Mendelssohn
Faith from Song Without Words

Page 61, No. 9

accelerando	becoming quicker
adagio	slow
mano destra	right hand
mano sinistra	left hand
prestissimo	as fast as possible
Tempo primo	return to the original tempo or speed
vivace	lively, quick

Page 61, No. 10

a. Who composed Young Persons Guide to the Orchestra? **Benjamin Britten**

b. In what country was he born? **England or Great Britain**

c. In what era did he live? **Modern**

d. Who composed the theme on which this work is based? **Henry Purcell**

e. What era did this composer live? **Baroque**

f. How many variations are in Young Persons Guide to the Orchestra? **13**

g. What are the four instrument families featured in this composition?

    1. **Strings**
    2. **Woodwinds**
    3. **Brass**
    4. **Percussion**

h. What type of piece is the final movement of this composition? **Fugue**

Page 64, No. 1

Page 65, No. 2

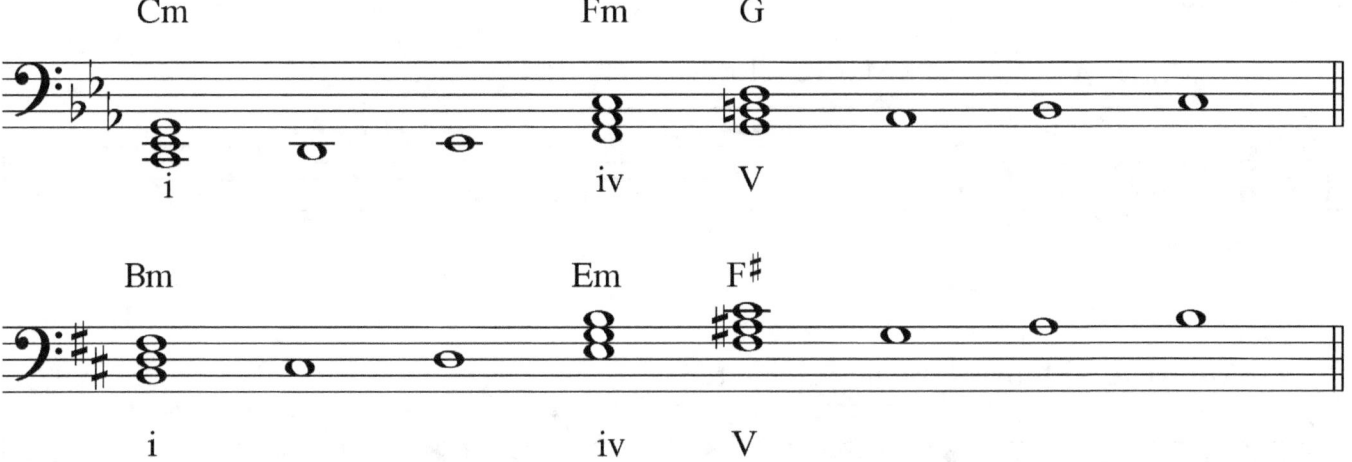

Page 68, No. 2

Page 68, No. 3

Key:	E minor	G minor	F# minor	C minor
Triad:	tonic	dominant	subdominant	tonic
	i	V	iv	i

Key:	B minor	D minor	F# minor	C minor
Triad:	dominant	subdominant	tonic	dominant
	V	iv	i	V

Page 69, No. 1

Page 70, No. 2

Page 73, No. 1 (other options are possible)

© San Marco Publications 2022 103 Level 4

Page 73, No. 2 (other options are possible)

Page 73, No. 3 (other options are possible)

Page 74, No. 4 (other options are possible)

Page 74, No. 5 (other options are possible)

Page 74, No. 6 (other options are possible)

© San Marco Publications 2022

Page 81, No. 1

Franz Schubert
Slumber Song

a. Add the time signature directly on the music.

b. Name the key of this piece. **G major**

c. Mark the phrases with slurs.

d. Label the phrases with *a*, *a¹*, and *b*.

e. Name the chord formed by the notes at A: **G major** B: **D major**

Piano Sonata, Mvt. I

Franz Joseph Haydn
(1732-1809)

a. Add the correct time signature directly on the music.

b. Name the key of this piece. **G major**

c. Name the composer of this piece. **Franz Joseph Haydn**

d. On which beat does this piece begin? **3**

e. Name the intervals at : A **maj 3** B **per 8** C **maj 6**

f. Does this piece end on a stable or unstable degree? **stable**

g. Explain the sign at D. **Repeat sign, repeat from the beginning**

h. Define *Presto* **Very fast**

i. Find one half step and circle it.

Page 83

Menuetto

Wolfgang Amadeus Mozart
(1756-1791)

a. Add the correct time signature directly on the music.

b. Name the key of this piece. **D major**

c. Name the composer of this piece. **Wolfgang Amadeus Mozart**

d. When did this composer live? **1756-1791**

e. Name the intervals at : A **per 4**   B **per 5**   C **maj 2**

f. Explain the sign at D. **slur, play the notes smoothly connected**

h. Define *andante*. **moderate walking pace**

i. Does this piece end on a stable or unstable scale degree? **stable**

j. Name the triad formed by the notes at E: **G major**

k. In this key, this triad is the: ❏ tonic triad   ☑ subdominant triad   ❏ dominant triad

© San Marco Publications 2022   107   Level 4

Page 84, No. 1 Review 3

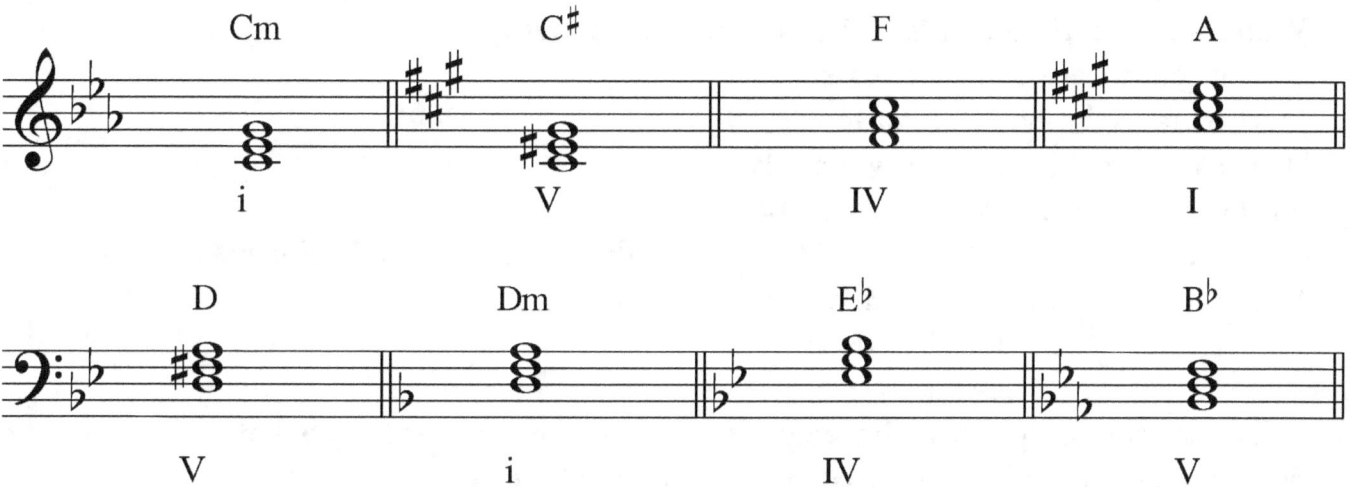

Page 84, No. 2

Key:	E♭ major	G major	A major	B♭ major
Triad:	tonic	dominant	subdominant	tonic
	I	V	IV	I

Page 85, No. 3

	D	F♯m	Gm	F♯
Key:	G minor	F♯ minor	D minor	B minor
Triad:	dominant	tonic	subdominant	dominant

Page 85, No. 4 (other options are possible)

Page 85, No. 5 (other options are possible)

Page 86, No. 6

a. Who composed *The Nutcracker*? **Piotr Ilyich Tchaikovsky**
b. In what country was he born? **Russia**
c. In what era did he live? **Romantic**
d. How many symphonies did he write? **Six**
e. What type of work is *The Nutcracker*? **Ballet**
f. Name a dance from *The Nutcracker*. **Waltz of the flowers, Dance of the Sugar Plum Fairy**
g. Who choreographed *The Nutcracker*?
        1. **Marius Petipa**
        2. **Lev Ivanov**
h. What is a choreographer? **A choreographer designs the dances for a ballet.**
i. What unique instrument is featured in *The Nutcracker*? **Celesta**

Page 87, No. 7

n) cantabile	a) becoming quicker
m) vivace	b) a slow tempo between andante and largo
i) rallentando	c) fairly fast, a little slower than allegro
o) dolce	d) fast
r) marcato	e) slow
l) Tempo primo	f) at a moderate tempo
e) adagio	g) very fast
j) ritardando	h) as fast as possible
c) allegretto	i) slowing down
h) prestissimo	j) slowing down gradually
p) grazioso	k) speed at which music is performed
f) moderato	l) return to the original tempo
g) presto	m) lively, brisk
a) accelerando	n) in a singing style
q) maestoso	o) sweetly
k) tempo	p) gracefully
d) allegro	q) majestically
b) lento	r) marked or stressed

www.ingramcontent.com/pod-product-compliance
Lightning Source LLC
Chambersburg PA
CBHW081621100526
44590CB00021B/3546